Britain Now
QUIZ

S0-DQX-354

Michael Williams

Longman Group Limited
*Longman House, Burnt Mill, Harlow,
Essex CM20 2JE, England
and Associated Companies throughout the world.*

© New Society 1985
*All rights reserved; no part of this publication
may be reproduced, stored in a retrieval system,
or transmitted in any form or by any means, electronic,
mechanical, photocopying, recording, or otherwise,
without the prior written permission of the Publishers.*

First published 1985

British Library Cataloguing in Publication Data

Williams, Michael
  British quiz.
  1. Great Britain–Social conditions–1945-–
  Examinations, questions, etc.
  I. Title
  941.085'8'076   HN385.5

ISBN 0-582-89231-7

Set in 10/11 pt 'Monophoto' Apollo by
Chambers Wallace Ltd, London
Printed in Great Britain by
Butler & Tanner Ltd, London & Frome

Contents

Introduction

THIS IS A BOOK of facts about the United Kingdom today. However, it won't tell you which is the longest railway tunnel, the deepest coal mine, or the rarest butterfly; rather, it is a snapshot of the lives of British people – how we spend our time, what we buy, how we vote, what we eat, the crimes we commit, how we organise our love lives, and what we do when we get old.

Much of the information here comes from official sources – the government and its departments pump out reams of information every week. Indeed there are three organisations – the Office of Population Censuses and Surveys, the Central Statistical Office, and the Business Statistics Office – whose principal job is to collate and produce data on behalf of the state. Other material comes from the large-scale opinion polling and market research organisations such as Gallup and the British Market Research Bureau. A third useful source has been the various independent social surveys that are carried out in universities, or in independent research organisations like the Policy Studies Institute. Despite the authority of the sources, however, all these statistics should be treated with a bit of caution.

Disraeli's famous assertion that statistics are somehow worse than lies was obviously an overstatement; but statistical information should certainly be read carefully if we are to appreciate exactly what it is telling us. For example, one of the commonest misreadings of statistics today is the idea that, because the overall birth rate of black Britons is higher than that of white people, then the country is in danger of being 'overrun'. This is demonstrably untrue. The simple statistics leave out the fact that the age structures of the two populations are very different. Because of the pattern of immigration, the black population at present is much younger than the white population and includes more women of childbearing age.

As well as the necessity of comparing like with like, it is also important to bear in mind 'other' factors. It happens to be true, for instance, that people who are moderate drinkers are less likely than teetotallers to take time off work. But does this mean that drinking makes you healthy? It could simply be that people are teetotal *because* they have health problems already. Remember, too, that 'rates' are different from absolute numbers. More people die crossing the road than practising hang-gliding. But this does not, of course, mean that hang-gliding is safer. The death rate for hang-gliding is simply higher, because fewer people take part.

Sources should also be carefully assessed – statistics about the mining industry, for example, bear different interpretations depending on whether they are presented by the National Union of Mineworkers or the National Coal Board. You would be well advised to read the figures produced both by the government *and* by Friends of the Earth before deciding what to believe about radiation leaks.

Some types of social statistics inevitably raise difficulties because they are, by their nature, incomplete. Crime statistics, for example, refer only to *recorded* crime, which is a very small proportion of total crime. It is officially reckoned that there are four times as many incidents of wounding and twelve times as many thefts from the person as every get recorded. Suicide figures are necessarily incomplete, too, since coroners will often deliberately try to avoid recording a suicide verdict, out of respect for the feelings of the victim's family.

We should also be wary of accepting at face value the answers to opinion surveys. These don't always tell the full story since we often don't known how, or by whom, the original questions were presented. One classic example of this was a survey into attitudes towards sex offenders. Of a sample of women, interviewed by women, 40 per cent thought that sex offenders should be publicly flogged, but the figure rose to 60 per cent when the women were interviewed by men. The interaction between the sexes had clearly affected the result in a way that hadn't been predicted.

I have tried to take all these factors into account in the wording of questions and answers in this book, and to eliminate anything that seems misleading. All the information given here refers to the United Kingdom (England, Wales, Scotland and Northern Ireland) except where otherwise stated. 'Britain' means England, Wales and Scotland only. Where dates are concerned, all figures are the latest available when this book went to press in summer 1984. I have only included a specific date when it seems specially interesting, where money is involved, or where figures are not part of an overall trend – terrorist offences in Northern Ireland, for example. Where there are multiple sources for an answer, I have often, for simplicity's sake, given only the main reference. Thus the Department of Health and Social Security sometimes also stands for the Scottish Health Service, the Welsh Office or the Department of Health and Social Security in Northern Ireland.

Finally, if anyone gets the bug to find out more about their society after using this book (and I hope many will), they could do no better than turn to the government's excellent publication, *Social Trends*, which in an ideal world would be on everyone's bookshelf, along with Roget, a good dictionary and the Bible. I have included a short introduction to other useful reading at the end of the book.

I would like to thank Paul Barker, Editor of *New Society*, who has published some of these questions in the magazine, and Alison Holding, who works for the Central Statistical Office, for reading the manuscript and providing invaluable advice. Rosa Barreto and Kate Lingard typed it expertly, mostly against the clock.

Michael Williams

Population

1 The population of the United Kingdom is some 56 million. Where does this put us in the world population league?

   (a) Fourteenth
   (b) Twenty-fourth
   (c) Thirty-fifth

2 Only once in this century in peacetime have there been more deaths than births in the United Kingdom, resulting in a population decrease. In which decade did this occur?

   (a) The 1920s
   (b) The 1970s
   (c) The 1980s

3 At the beginning of the 1960s, the average size of a household in Britain was just over three people. Is it more or less than this now?

4 More boys are born than girls. True or false?

5 How many widows are there for every widower in Britain?

   (a) Two
   (b) Three
   (c) Four

Answers   **Population**

1   The United Kingdom has the fourteenth largest population in the world. (Source, *Britain 1984*.)

2   The population temporarily decreased in the 1970s – between 1976 and 1977. Current projections are for a modest growth in the population, up to about 58 million in 2001. (Source, Office of Population Censuses and Surveys.)

3   It is less – the average household size is now 2.64 people. (Source, Office of Population Censuses and Surveys.)

4   True, but more men die each year than women, so from about the age of 50 women start to outnumber men. (Source, Office of Population Censuses and Surveys.)

5   There are four widows for every widower in Britain – 3.2 million, compared with 0.8 million. The ratio rises to five to one among those aged 65 or over. (Source, Office of Population Censuses and Surveys.)

Birth

1   How long, on average, does a couple wait between getting
    married and having their first child?

    (a)   Six months
    (b)   One-and-a-half years
    (c)   Two-and-a-half years

2   Some 40 per cent of pregnancies conceived outside
    marriage are terminated by legal abortion. How many
    pregnancies conceived within marriage end in legal
    abortion?

    (a)   1 per cent
    (b)   2 per cent
    (c)   8 per cent

3   Is it true that the baby of a mother aged between 16 and 19
    is more likely to die in the first year of life than the baby
    of a mother over 35?

4   In which month of the year do most births take place?

5   Working class parents are more likely to have large
    families than people in higher socio-economic groups. Is
    this still true?

Answers Birth

1   Two-and-a-half years. The median interval between
    marriage and first legitimate live birth is 29 months.
    (Statistically, the median is a particular kind of average:
    in this case there are as many births above the median as
    there are below it.) (Source, Office of Population Censuses
    and Surveys.)

2   About 8 per cent of pregnancies conceived within marriage
    end in abortion. (Source, *Britain 1984*.)

3   It is true. The infant mortality rate for children of mothers
    aged between 16 and 19 was 17.5 per 1,000 live births in
    1980. For women aged 35 and over, it was 11.5. (Source,
    Office of Population Censuses and Surveys.)

4   There are usually most births in March. The main peak of
    births is in the spring, though there is another peak at the
    end of September. (Source, Office of Population Censuses
    and Surveys.)

5   It is still true that the working classes have larger
    families. Families with fathers in unskilled or semi-skilled
    occupations include the highest proportion of fourth and
    subsequent children. (Source, Office of Population
    Censuses and Surveys.)

Marriage

1   What proportion of women aged 16 and over have never
    been married?

    (a)   21 per cent
    (b)   12 per cent
    (c)   2 per cent

2   In what percentage of married couples of working age
    does the wife have a job?

    (a)   10 per cent
    (b)   30 per cent
    (c)   60 per cent

3   At what age is a man most likely to enter into his first
    marriage?

    (a)   21
    (b)   24
    (c)   25

4   What proportion of women between 18 and 49 are
    cohabiting – that is, living with a man as his wife, but
    without a legal marriage tie?

5   In what proportion of married couples in England and
    Wales are both the husband and wife in each case in their
    first marriage?

    (a)   Nine out of ten
    (b)   Seven out of ten
    (c)   Five out of ten

Answers   **Marriage**

1   21 per cent of women of 16 and over have never been married. (Source, Office of Population Censuses and Surveys.)

2   Nearly 60 per cent of wives of working age have a job. (Source, *General Household Survey*.)

3   The age at which a single man is most likely to enter into marriage is 24 years. The age for remarriage by a divorced man is about 35 and for a widower, about 60. These are median ages – i.e. midway between the highest and the lowest. (Source, Office of Population Censuses and Surveys.)

4   4 per cent of women aged between 18 and 49 are cohabiting. (Source, *General Household Survey*.)

5   In 9 out of 10 couples (87 per cent), both husband and wife are in their first marriage. (Source, Office of Population Censuses and Surveys.)

Death

1   Deaths officially recorded as suicide are currently about
    5,000 a year. In what month are people most likely to
    commit suicide?

    (a)   January
    (b)   April
    (c)   August
    (d)   December

2   How many people would you expect to die in one year in
    a town with a population of 6,000? (Buckingham and
    Marlborough, in Wiltshire, are examples of towns of this
    size.)

    (a)   6
    (b)   34
    (c)   72

3   Which is the more common cause of death, circulatory
    disease (heart attacks, strokes etc.) or cancer?

4   How many more years can a man of three-score years and
    ten expect to live?

    (a)   No more years
    (b)   Two years
    (c)   Ten years

5   There are more than 1,000 cot deaths in England and
    Wales each year. Are boys or girls most likely to be
    affected?

Answers Death

1 April really is the cruellest month, accounting for the highest number of suicides every year. The low point is between September and November. (Source, Office of Health Economics.)

2 You could expect 72 people to die, since the number of deaths per 1,000 population in the United Kingdom is approximately 12. (Source, Office of Population Censuses and Surveys.)

3 Circulatory diseases are the biggest single cause of death, accounting for about half the number of deaths in the United Kingdom each year. Cancer accounts for between one-fifth and one quarter. (Source, Office of Population Censuses and Surveys.)

4 He can expect to live a further ten years. (Source, Government Actuary's Department.)

5 Boys are more likely to suffer from 'sudden infant death' – the so-called cot-death syndrome. (Source, Office of Population Censuses and Surveys.)

Migration

1   More people emigrate from the United Kingdom than enter as immigrants. True or false?

2   Between 800 and 1,000 people are deported from the United Kingdom each year. Are most of these people of foreign nationality or are they Commonwealth citizens?

3   In order to become a naturalized citizen of the United Kingdom, it is necessary to have lived here for five years and to be of 'good character'. It is also necessary to have 'sufficient knowledge' of one of three languages. Which languages?

4   Which is the most popular destination for people emigrating?

    (a)   The 'old Commonwealth' – Australia, Canada, New Zealand
    (b)   South Africa
    (c)   EEC countries
    (d)   The United States

5   What proportion of immigrants to the United Kingdom come from the Caribbean?

    (a)   One in 5
    (b)   One in 15
    (c)   One in 50

Answers Migration

1. True. In the decade up to 1981 there was a net loss of nearly 0.4 million people from the United Kingdom through migration. There were 1.9 million immigrants compared with 2.2 million emigrants. (Source, Office of Population Censuses and Surveys.)

2. Most deportations are of Commonwealth citizens. In 1983, 492 were deported compared with 367 foreign nationals. (Source, Home Office.)

3. The languages are English, Welsh or Scottish Gaelic. (Source, *Britain 1984*.)

4. The 'old Commonwealth' countries are the most popular destination, taking 79,000 emigrants in 1981, compared with 28,000 going to EEC countries, the next most popular destination. (Source, Office of Population Censuses and Surveys.)

5. Approximately one in 50 immigrants comes from the Caribbean. In 1981 there were 153,000 immigrants in all, of whom 3,000 came from the Caribbean New Commonwealth. (Source, Office of Population Censuses and Surveys.)

Families

1   Married couples with dependent children account for
    more than half the families in Britain. True or false?

2   In Britain, how many mothers with a youngest child under
    five have a full-time job?

    (a)   One in 16
    (b)   One in 60
    (c)   One in 600

3   Who is the person most likely to look after a working
    mother's pre-school age children while she is at work?

    (a)   Husband
    (b)   Grandmother
    (c)   Childminder in her own home
    (d)   Nanny in the mother's home

4   The percentage of people in households living alone more
    than doubled between 1961 and 1982 – from 4 per cent to
    9 per cent. Who is more likely to live alone, a person aged
    between 16 and 24 or a person in the age range 65 to 74?

5   What proportion of families in Britain with dependent
    children are headed by single parents?

    (a)   3 per cent
    (b)   4 per cent
    (c)   13 per cent

Answers Families

1   It is false. Married couples with dependent children account for two-fifths of families. (Source, Office of Population Censuses and Surveys.)

2   One in 16 mothers with a youngest child under five has a full-time job. (Source, *General Household Survey*.)

3   The husband looks after the children in the majority of cases (47 per cent). Otherwise, it is most likely to be a grandmother (34 per cent), less frequently a childminder (16 per cent). In only 4 per cent of cases is a nanny employed. (Source, Department of Employment.)

4   People aged between 65 and 74 are far more likely to live alone. In this age group 15 per cent of men and 37 per cent of women live alone. The figure for the 16 to 24s is 0.9 per cent. (Source, Office of Population Censuses and Surveys.)

5   A total of 13 per cent of families with dependent children in Britain are single-parent families. At the beginning of the 1970s, this figure was only 8 per cent. (Source, *General Household Survey*.)

The elderly

1 Between now and the end of the century there will be a big change in the proportion of people aged between 65 and 74 in the elderly population. Will there be more in this age group, or fewer?

2 Which of these statements is true?

   (a) People aged 61 or over are more likely to experience assault or theft from the person than any other age group.
   (b) People aged 61 or over are less likely to experience assault or theft from the person than any other age group.

3 Twenty-five years ago, more than a quarter of all the men in Britain over retirement age were still working. How many men over 65 have jobs today?

   (a) 27 per cent
   (b) 17 per cent
   (c) 7 per cent

4 In what kind of situation is the average woman aged over 65 most likely to be living?

   (a) On her own
   (b) With one other person
   (c) In an old people's home
   (d) In a household with two or more other people

5 At the end of the 1950s, only 9 per cent of people over 65 in Britain lived in households with this modern convenience. Now 64 per cent do. What is it?

   (a) A car
   (b) A washing machine
   (c) A telephone
   (d) An electric blanket

Answers   The elderly

1   The proportion of 65- to 74-year-olds in the United
    Kingdom will decrease – from 62 per cent of the over-65
    population in 1981 to 53 per cent in 2001. (Source, Office
    of Population Censuses and Surveys.)

2   The second statement is true. Elderly people are least likely
    to be victims of either of these crimes. Both offences are
    most likely to be experienced by people aged 30 or under.
    (Source, Home Office.)

3   Only 7 per cent of men over retirement age have jobs.
    3 per cent are still in full-time work and 4 per cent have
    part-time jobs. (Source, *Social Trends*, 1984.)

4   A woman over 65 is most likely to be living on her own.
    Some 46 per cent of women over 65 in private households
    in Britain live on their own, compared with 44 per cent
    who live with one other person. Only about 10 per cent
    live in households with more than two other people, and
    the number who live in old people's homes is very small –
    fewer than 200,000. (Source, *Social Trends*, 1984.)

5   It is a telephone. Access to cars among the elderly has
    increased much more slowly – from 16 per cent to 36 per
    cent. (Source, *Social Trends*, 1984.)

Divorce

1 In 1961, there were roughly two divorces for every 1,000
married couples. What is the figure now?

   (a) 4
   (b) 12
   (c) 56

2 How many divorces take place before the fourth wedding
anniversary?

   (a) 2 per cent
   (b) 6 per cent
   (c) 12 per cent

3 A divorced person who has remarried is much less likely
to divorce, in the second or subsequent marriage, than a
person of similar age married for the first time. Is this
true?

4 If a woman is divorced before the age of 35, what are her
chances of remarrying within six years?

   (a) One in 50
   (b) One in 10
   (c) One in 2

5 Among couples who get divorced in England and Wales,
is the marriage likely to have lasted longer if the couple do
or do not have children under 16?

Answers **Divorce**

1   There are currently 12 divorces in one year for every
    1,000 married couples. There are regional variations,
    however, with lower figures in Scotland and Northern
    Ireland. (Source, *Britain 1984*.)

2   Some 12 per cent of divorces in Britain take place before
    the fourth wedding anniversary. Of the total number of
    divorces, about half take place within the first ten years
    of marriage. (Source, Office of Population Censuses and
    Surveys.)

3   It is not true. A divorced woman who remarries is
    approximately twice as likely to divorce as a single woman
    who gets married at the same age. A remarried man is
    one-and-a-half times as likely to divorce as his
    counterpart in a first marriage. (Source, Office of
    Population Censuses and Surveys.)

4   There is roughly a one in two chance that she will remarry
    within this time. Some 23 per cent remarry within three
    years and 52 per cent within six years. (Source, *General
    Household Survey*.)

5   A marriage is likely to have lasted longer if the couple
    have children under 16. The average duration under these
    circumstances is 11 years, compared to eight years for the
    rest of divorcing couples. (Source, *Social Trends*, 1984.)

Children

1   The majority of five-year-olds in Britain today are the
    only child of their family. True or false?

2   More than 40,000 children come into care in England and
    Wales each year. What is the most common reason for
    this?

    (a)   The child has committed an offence
    (b)   The parents are ill, or having a baby
    (c)   The parents have separated or divorced
    (d)   The home conditions are unsatisfactory

3   Women in the professional classes are less likely to
    breastfeed their babies than working class women. Is
    this true?

4   What is happening to the numbers of children of pre-
    school age in the United Kingdom? Are they:

    (a)   Increasing?
    (b)   Decreasing?
    (c)   Staying about the same?

5   How much pocket money is the average five- to seven-
    year-old given each week?

    (a)   16p
    (b)   23p
    (c)   71p

Answers Children

1   It is false. Only one child in ten is an only child at the age of five. (Source, Child Health and Education Study.)

2   The most common reason for children coming into care in England and Wales is the short-term illness of a parent or confinement of the mother. These temporary conditions accounted for just over 20 per cent of cases in 1981. (Source, Department of Health and Social Security.)

3   It is not true. In England and Wales, nearly 90 per cent of women whose husbands are in professional occupations breastfeed their babies, compared with just over 50 per cent of women whose husbands are partly skilled or unskilled. (Source, Office of Population Censuses and Surveys.)

4   The number of pre-school-age children is on the increase, and is expected to remain so throughout the 1980s. (Source, Office of Population Censuses and Surveys.)

5   The average amount given to a five- to seven-year-old was 71p in 1983. A total of £640 million was given in pocket money to Britain's nine million five- to 16-year-olds. (Source, *Walls Ice Cream Survey,* 1983.)

Education

1   Over half of all school leavers in Britain have at least one
    GCE O-level, grade A-C. True or false?

2   Which O-level subject has the lowest pass rate for boys:
    metalwork, woodwork or sociology?

3   Which of these types of state school has the smallest
    number of pupils per teacher?

    (a)   Nursery schools
    (b)   Primary schools
    (c)   Secondary schools

4   How many employed people in Britain have no
    educational qualifications at all?

    (a)   One in ten
    (b)   Two in ten
    (c)   Four in ten

5   Some 10.4 million children attend the United Kingdom's
    35,000 schools. What proportion go to schools that are
    not maintained in some way by the state?

    (a)   0.5 per cent
    (b)   6 per cent
    (c)   12 per cent

Answers Education

1 It is true that over half the school-leavers in Britain (55 per cent) have at least one GCE O-level grade A-C, or equivalent. (Source, Department of Education and Science.)

2 Sociology has the lowest pass rate of the three. (Source, the *Sunday Times*.)

3 Secondary schools, which have a ratio of 16 pupils per teacher, compared with 22 in both nursery and primary schools. (Source, Department of Education and Science.)

4 Four in ten employed people in Britain have no educational qualifications at all. The figures are directly related to age: about six in ten of the 50 to 59 age group have no qualifications, compared with approximately two in ten of the 16 to 19s. (Source, Department of Employment.)

5 Some 6 per cent of pupils attend schools wholly independent of direct public financial support. (Source, *Britain 1984*.)

Higher education

1   Which of these subject areas accounts for most of the
    university first degrees awarded in the United Kingdom?

    (a)   Engineering and technology
    (b)   Social, administrative and business studies
    (c)   Languages

2   What proportion of university and college students come
    from unskilled or semi-skilled working class backgrounds?

    (a)   A half
    (b)   A quarter
    (c)   One-tenth

3   Which county has the largest proportion of people with
    higher educational qualifications among its employed
    population?

    (a)   Oxfordshire
    (b)   Cambridgeshire
    (c)   Greater London

4   Which is the most common destination for people
    graduating from a university with a first degree?

    (a)   Industry
    (b)   Commerce
    (c)   Further education or training
    (d)   Unemployment

5   Of approximately 70,000 university first degrees awarded
    each year in the United Kingdom, what percentage goes
    to women?

    (a)   24 per cent
    (b)   29 per cent
    (c)   38 per cent

Answers **Higher education**

1   Social, administrative and business studies account for the most degrees – 25 per cent of those obtained by men and 28 per cent by women. This compares with 22 and 2 per cent respectively in the field of engineering and technology. (Source, University Grants Committee.)

2   One-tenth of students at universities, polytechnics and colleges of further education in Britain come from a family where the father is in unskilled or semi-skilled manual work. Nearly half the student total are from a background with a father who is in professional work, or is an employer or manager. (Source, *General Household Survey.*)

3   Oxfordshire has the highest proportion, with 18 per cent of male employees having higher educational qualifications and 16 per cent of female employees. This compares with 15 and 13 per cent in Cambridgeshire and 15 and 14 per cent in Greater London. (Source, *Regional Trends,* 1984.)

4   Further education and training is the most common single destination, accounting for just over a quarter of graduates. Unemployment accounts for about an eighth. (Source, University Grants Committee.)

5   Thirty-eight per cent of university first degrees go to women. (Source, University Grants Committee.)

Work

1   Less than half the population of the United Kingdom is in employment. True or false?

2   Where in Britain does the average worker get the lowest pay?

(a)   The east midlands
(b)   Scotland
(c)   The north

3   In which of these jobs would you be likely to work the most overtime?

(a)   Postman
(b)   Railway porter
(c)   Baker

4   How many minutes does it take the average manual worker to earn enough, after tax, to buy a standard loaf of sliced bread?

5   In which industry would you be most likely to do shiftwork?

(a)   Medical and health services
(b)   Motor vehicles and parts
(c)   Mineral oil processing

Answers Work

1   It is true. Only some two-fifths of the total population is in employment. (Source, *Hansard*.)

2   The east midlands, where pay for full-time workers is three-quarters of the London average. (Source, New Earnings Survey, 1983.)

3   A railway porter would expect to work the most overtime – 12.7 hours a week on average. A postman would work 6.7 hours and a baker 7.4. (Source, New Earnings Survey, 1983.)

4   It takes the average manual worker approximately nine minutes to earn enough to buy a standard loaf of sliced bread. (Source, *Hansard*.)

5   Mineral oil processing. (Source, New Earnings Survey, 1983.)

Unemployment

1 When was the last time unemployment was below one million?

   (a)   1955
   (b)   1965
   (c)   1975

2 How much more likely is an unskilled man to be out of work than a professional man?

   (a)   Twice as likely
   (b)   Three times as likely
   (c)   Ten times as likely

3 How is an unemployed man most likely to spend his afternoons?

   (a)   Job hunting
   (b)   Watching television
   (c)   Doing housework
   (d)   Doing nothing/sitting around

4 Has unemployment been increasing more rapidly among men or among women?

5 Which ethnic group suffers the highest male unemployment rate?

   (a)   People of West Indian origin
   (b)   People of Indian/Pakistani/Bangladeshi origin

Answers   Unemployment

1   The last time unemployment was below one million was 1975. (Source, Department of Employment.)

2   An unskilled man is ten times more likely to be unemployed than is a professional man, according to figures from the 1981 census. (Source, Office of Population Censuses and Surveys.)

3   An unemployed man in Britain is most likely to spend his afternoons watching television. This is the occupation of 14 per cent of unemployed males, compared with 7 per cent who do the housework, 12 per cent who go job hunting and 9 per cent who do nothing or sit around. (Source, Economist Intelligence Unit.)

4   Unemployment has increased more rapidly among women than among men. Between 1980 and 1984 the number of unemployed male claimants increased by 125 per cent, while the number of females increased by 141 per cent. (Source, *Hansard.*)

5   The West Indian group suffers most, with 21 per cent of economically active males between 16 and 64 unemployed in 1981. The figures for Indian/Pakistani/Bangladeshi men, and white men were 17 per cent and 10 per cent respectively. (Source, *Social Trends,* 1984.)

Resources

1   In which activity do we use the most water?

    (a)   Using a washing machine
    (b)   Flushing the lavatory
    (c)   Bathing

2   As well as coal and oil, the United Kingdom has several other profitable, non-fuel minerals. Which is the most valuable, in terms of the amount produced in a year?

    (a)   Tin
    (b)   Sand and gravel
    (c)   Salt
    (d)   Gypsum and anhydrite

3   Less than 2.5 per cent of the United Kingdom's labour force works in agriculture. How much of its own food is this country able to produce?

    (a)   One-tenth
    (b)   A half
    (c)   Two-thirds

4   Woodland covers about 7 per cent of England, 12 per cent of Scotland and 11 per cent of Wales. How much of our requirement for timber and timber products do we need to import?

    (a)   7 per cent
    (b)   34 per cent
    (c)   90 per cent

5   Which do British farmers have most of, cattle, sheep or pigs?

Answers **Resources**

1   Of the 120 litres the average person in England and Wales uses each day, by far the largest amount (32 per cent) is used in flushing lavatories. Seventeen per cent is used in baths and showers and 12 per cent in washing machines. (Source, Department of the Environment.)

2   Sand and gravel are the most valuable, together producing £329 million in 1981. Tin produced £20 million, salt £49 million, and gypsum and anhydrite £15 million. (Source, *Britain 1984.*)

3   The United Kingdom produces some two-thirds of its own food, despite having a lower proportion of the workforce engaged in agriculture than any other major industrial country. (Source, *Britain 1984.*)

4   The United Kingdom needs to import over 90 per cent of the timber and timber products it uses. (Source, *Britain 1984.*)

5   There are more sheep and lambs (33 million) in the United Kingdom, than cattle (13 million) and pigs (8 million) put together. (Source, Ministry of Agriculture, Fisheries and Food.)

The economy and trade

1   The United Kingdom's traditional economic strength,
    since the Industrial Revolution, has been based on
    manufacturing. How many of the employed labour force
    work in manufacturing today?

    (a)   One in two
    (b)   One in four
    (c)   Three in four

2   The United Kingdom exports a greater proportion of its
    total output of goods and services than do either the
    United States or Japan. True or false?

3   Where do we send most of our visible exports (i.e., goods
    and products)? Do they go to other Commonwealth
    countries, or to countries in the EEC?

4   Which country provides our biggest export market?

    (a)   The United States
    (b)   Saudi Arabia
    (c)   Nigeria
    (d)   The Irish Republic

5   There are some 60 companies with net assets of over £500
    million registered in the United Kingdom. In what line of
    business are the top two companies?

    (a)   Tobacco
    (b)   Oil
    (c)   Motor cars
    (d)   Chemicals

Answers   **The economy and trade**

1   One in four – some 27 per cent – of the employed labour force currently works in manufacturing. (Source, *Britain 1984*.)

2   It is true. We export about 30 per cent of our goods and services altogether. The only comparable developed countries that can match this total are Italy and West Germany. (Source, *Britain 1984*.)

3   Most of our visible exports go to EEC countries. They took 42 per cent in 1982, compared with 13 per cent taken by Commonwealth countries. (Source, *Britain 1984*.)

4   The United States is our largest single export market, taking some 13 per cent of British exports. The second biggest single export market is West Germany. (Source, Department of Trade.)

5   The two top companies are both concerned with oil. They are: British Petroleum, with a turnover in 1981-82 of £34,583 million, and Shell Transport and Trading (£21,910 million turnover.) (Source, *Britain 1984*.)

Money

1 How do the majority of manual workers in Britain receive their wages?

(a) In cash
(b) By cheque
(c) By bank credit

2 Which of these banknotes has the highest total value in terms of notes in circulation?

(a) The £5 note
(b) The £10 note
(c) The £50 note

3 Half of us have savings in building societies. How many of us own premium bonds?

(a) One-twentieth
(b) One-tenth
(c) One-third

Are Scottish banknotes legal tender in England?

How much did it require in 1983 to buy what £1 could purchase in 1973?

(a) £1.82
(b) £2.34
(c) £3.58

Answers Money

1 Most manual workers still get their wages in cash – some 68 per cent were paid this way in 1981. (Source, Inter-Bank Research Organisation.)

2 The value of £10 notes in circulation is highest, at £4,530,629,280 (1983 figures). The value of £5 notes in circulation in 1983 was £2,849,809,545, and of £50 notes, £632,699,050. (Source, *Whitaker's Almanack*.)

3 Approximately one-third of us own some premium bonds. (Source, British Market Research Bureau.)

4 No. They are not legal tender anywhere in the United Kingdom, but in practice they are accepted by most banks. (Source, Bank of England.)

5 Compared with 1983, the pound in 1973 had a value of £3.58. (Source, Central Statistical Office.)

Wealth

1   The largest slice of marketable wealth owned by the average Briton is a house. Which is the next largest?

   (a)   Stocks and shares
   (b)   Consumer durables
   (c)   Bank and National Savings deposits

2   The government and its agencies own about 20 per cent of the total land in the United Kingdom. How much is still owned by the landed aristocracy?

   (a)   2 per cent
   (b)   13 per cent
   (c)   40 per cent

3   How much of the marketable wealth in the United Kingdom (shares, bank deposits, houses, consumer durables, etc.) is owned by the richest 1 per cent of the population?

   (a)   5 per cent
   (b)   12 per cent
   (c)   23 per cent

4   How much of the total marketable wealth in the United Kingdom is owned by the poorest 50 per cent of the population?

   (a)   6 per cent
   (b)   23 per cent
   (c)   30 per cent

5   In 1971, stocks and shares represented 25 per cent of the marketable wealth owned by individuals in the United Kingdom. What proportion did they account for ten years later?

   (a)   34 per cent
   (b)   11 per cent
   (c)   9 per cent

Answers Wealth

1 After housing, consumer durables represent the biggest slice of marketable wealth owned by the average Briton. (Source, Central Statistical Office.)

2 More than 40 per cent of all land is owned by the landed aristocracy. (Source, Counter Information Services.)

3 The richest 1 per cent owns 23 per cent of marketable wealth in the United Kingdom. (Source, Inland Revenue.)

4 The poorest 50 per cent of the population owns 6 per cent of marketable wealth. (Source, Inland Revenue.)

5 In 1981, stocks and shares accounted for 9 per cent of the marketable wealth of individuals. (Source, Inland Revenue.)

Poverty

1   When the welfare state was founded in 1948, one person
    in 33 was dependent on supplementary benefit (national
    assistance as it was known then). How many are
    dependent on supplementary benefit today?

    (a)   One in 8
    (b)   One in 17
    (c)   One in 42

2   Which of these things is most likely to be lacked by people
    in the United Kingdom today?

    (a)   A damp-free house
    (b)   Two pairs of all-weather shoes
    (c)   A roast joint, or the equivalent, once a week
    (d)   Self-contained accommodation.

3   A common statistical definition of people with low
    incomes is 'people living on incomes up to 140 per cent
    of their supplementary benefit entitlement'. How many
    people fall into this category?

    (a)   One in 4
    (b)   One in 16
    (c)   One in 64

4   Most of the people living on incomes below the level
    where supplementary benefit applies are of pension age.
    True or false?

5   Which of these groups has most members living below
    supplementary benefit level?

    (a)   People in full-time work
    (b)   People unemployed for more than three months
    (c)   People sick or disabled for more than three months

Answers   Poverty

1   One person in eight is dependent on supplementary benefit today. (Source, Child Poverty Action Group.)

2   People are least likely to have two pairs of all-weather shoes. These are lacked by 11 per cent of the population. (Source, London Weekend Television/MORI.)

3   One in four of the population – about 15 million people – is living on an income below 140 per cent of supplementary benefit level. (Source, Child Poverty Action Group/ Department of Health and Social Security.)

4   It is false. In 1981, there were 1,120,000 people of pension age living below supplementary benefit level, compared with 1,690,000 people under pension age. (Source, Child Poverty Action Group/Department of Health and Social Security.)

5   People in full-time work comprise the biggest group of those living below supplementary benefit level – 680,000 in 1981, compared with 480,000 people who have been unemployed for more than three months. (Source, Child Poverty Action Group/Department of Health and Social Security.)

Incomes

1   Between 1970 and 1982, average earnings for full-time
    male employees in Britain increased fivefold, from £29 to
    £150 a week. What happened to women's earnings?

    (a)   They doubled
    (b)   They trebled
    (c)   They increased sixfold

2   Who has the highest income?

    (a)   The Commissioner of the Metropolitan Police
    (b)   The Archbishop of Canterbury
    (c)   The Secretary of State for Defence
    (d)   The Lord Chief Justice

3   All these occupations feature in the top ten best-paid
    manual jobs. Rank them in order of pay:

    (a)   Crane drivers
    (b)   Gas fitters
    (c)   Miners (face workers)
    (d)   Printing machine minders
    (e)   Steel erectors

4   Underground miners are among the best paid manual
    workers. Do they earn more or less than the average non-
    manual wage?

5   Who, on average, earns most, a police sergeant or an
    architect?

Answers Incomes

1   The average earnings of full-time female employees
    increased sixfold over the period – from £16 to £99 a week.
    (Source, *Social Trends,* 1984.)

2   The Lord Chief Justice has the highest income – a total of
    £56,500 a year in 1983. The Metropolitan Police
    Commissioner is next, with £40,500, followed by the
    Secretary of State for Defence (£38,910) and the
    Archbishop of Canterbury (£22,930). (Source, *Whitaker's
    Almanack.*)

3   The correct order is: Miners, gas fitters, printers, steel
    erectors, crane drivers. (Source, New Earnings Survey,
    1983.)

4   Miners earn approximately 1 per cent less than the
    average non-manual wage. (Source, New Earnings
    Survey, 1983.)

5   A police sergeant (£250 a week gross in 1983) earns more
    than an architect (£223 a week). (Source, New Earnings
    Survey, 1983.)

The public purse

1 Which is the largest of these public sector corporations, in terms of annual turnover?

   (a) The British Steel Corporation
   (b) The British Gas Corporation
   (c) The Electricity Council and boards

2 Which of these government departments employs the most civil servants?

   (a) Employment
   (b) Education and Science
   (c) Environment

3 Which of these sources of tax provides most money for the government?

   (a) Car tax
   (b) Tax on tobacco
   (c) Betting and gaming tax
   (d) Capital transfer tax

4 If the money used annually to maintain the monarchy were diverted to road building, how many miles of motorway could be built?

5 On which do we as a nation spend most?

   (a) Defence
   (b) The National Health Service
   (c) Social security benefits

Answers The public purse

1   The Electricity Council and boards have the biggest turnover, at £8,417 million in the financial year 1982-83. (Source, *Britain 1984*.)

2   Employment is the biggest department, with 57,900 staff in mid-1983. Education and Science had 3,500 and Environment 39,400. (Source, HM Treasury.)

3   Tax on tobacco provides the greatest amount – 4.2 per cent of total tax income in 1983-84. Car tax produces 0.7 per cent of total income, as does betting tax. Capital transfer tax provides 0.6 per cent. (Source, *Britain 1984*.)

4   Approximately three-and-a-half miles of motorway could be built for the annual cost of the British monarchy. (Source, *The Times*.)

5   We spend most on social security benefits – more than twice as much (£31,900 million in 1982) as on the National Health Service (£14,000 million) and defence (£14,500 million). (Source, Ministry of Defence.)

Choice

1   For what kind of entertainment does the average
household spend most on admission tickets?

    (a)   Cinema
    (b)   Theatre and concerts
    (c)   Dances
    (d)   Football matches

2   Which are we more likely to grow in our gardens, grass or
flowers?

3   Most British women go out to work because they feel they
have to, rather than because they enjoy it. True or false?

4   In how much of the mail we send do we bother to include
the postcode in the address?

    (a)   93 per cent
    (b)   84 per cent
    (c)   56 per cent

5   The average family uses 90 toilet rolls in one year. How
many of us buy hard toilet paper in preference to soft?

    (a)   One in 3
    (b)   One in 10
    (c)   One in 50

Answers Choice

1   The average household spends most on admissions to theatre and concerts – 18p a week in 1982, compared with 12p for dances, 10p for cinemas and 6p for football matches. (Source, Family Expenditure Survey.)

2   We are slightly more likely (74 per cent of us) to grow flowers in our gardens than grass (73 per cent). Some 38 per cent grow vegetables and 32 per cent fruit. (Source, British Market Research Bureau.)

3   It is false. According to *Women and Employment,* a major survey published by the Department of Employment and the Office of Population Censuses and Surveys in 1984, a majority of women said they enjoyed working. Only 6 per cent said they definitely did not enjoy working.

4   About 56 per cent of the mail sent includes the postcode. (Source, *Hansard.*)

5   Only one person in 50 prefers hard toilet paper to soft. (Source, *Labour Research.*)

Food

1   In the past 20 years, consumption of all except one of
    these foods has declined. Which is it?

    (a) Eggs
    (b) Beef
    (c) Poultry
    (d) Potatoes
    (e) Butter

2   How many households have milk delivered to their
    doorstep?

    (a) Four in ten
    (b) Five in ten
    (c) Nine in ten

3   The United Kingdom is among the world's top ten
    producers of this food. Also in the top ten are China, East
    Germany, Poland, the Soviet Union and the United
    States. What is the food?

    (a) Cabbage
    (b) Baked beans
    (c) Apples
    (d) Potatoes

4   The Italians may have invented ice cream, but the British
    eat more of it. Is this true?

5   Which do we as a nation spend more on?

    (a) Restaurant meals
    (b) Take-away meals and snacks
    (c) School and canteen meals

Answers   Food

1   Poultry is the only category in which consumption has increased. Butter has suffered the most dramatic decline – consumption almost halved between 1961 and 1982. (Source, National Food Survey.)

2   Nine out of ten households in the United Kingdom have doorstep deliveries of milk. With an average annual consumption of 116 litres a head, we are among the biggest milk-drinkers in the world. (Source, *Britain 1984*.)

3   Potatoes. The United Kingdom is ninth in the world league of potato-producing nations. The Soviet Union is top. (Source, *The Book of International Lists* by George Kurian, Macmillan 1981.)

4   It is true. Each person eats, on average, 85 ice creams a year, which adds up to 5.7 litres of ice cream for every man, woman and child. The Italians consume only four litres per person. (Source, Lyons Maid.)

5   Restaurant meals. Spending on meals outside the home accounted for a 'weight' of 36 out of 1,000 in the Retail Price Index in 1984. This breaks down as follows: restaurant meals, 20; take-away meals, 7; canteen and school meals, 9. (Source, *Hansard*.)

Shopping

1 Which item of clothing are men most likely to buy in any one year?

    (a) Shoes
    (b) Socks
    (c) Trousers
    (d) Jeans
    (e) Jumpers

2 Which are there most of in the United Kingdom?

    (a) Butchers' shops
    (b) Bakers' shops
    (c) Greengrocers' and fruiterers' shops

3 There are about one million vending machines selling commodities in the United Kingdom. On what do we spend most using coins in the slot?

    (a) Contraceptives
    (b) Sweets
    (c) Cigarettes
    (d) Canned and bottled drinks

4 What do most people in the United Kingdom feel about shopping for food in supermarkets?

    (a) They enjoy it
    (b) They tolerate it
    (c) They actively dislike it

5 Which of these items is most likely to be on the average shopping list?

    (a) Insecticide
    (b) Air freshener
    (c) Lavatory cleaner and bleach
    (d) Floor polish

Answers Shopping

1   Shoes are the most common buy, with only 29 per cent of
    men spending nothing on shoes in a year. Socks are the
    next most common buy, followed by trousers, jumpers
    and jeans, in that order. (Source, British Market Research
    Bureau.)

2   There are more butchers' shops (approximately 21,000)
    than bakers or greengrocers, which account for some
    13,000 and 15,000 shops respectively. (Source,
    Euromonitor.)

3   We spend most on cigarettes in vending machines – £350
    million in 1981, compared with £110 million spent in this
    way on confectionery. (Source, Euromonitor.)

4   Most people (46 per cent) actively dislike supermarket
    shopping; some 22 per cent get some degree of enjoyment
    and the rest merely tolerate it. The group most likely to
    enjoy shopping are the over-45s; those least likely are
    people in the south of England and those with children
    under ten. (Source, *How and Why Shoppers Buy,* a survey
    carried out for *Marketing* magazine.)

5   Lavatory cleaner and bleach are most likely to be on a
    shopping list, being used by 97 per cent of housewives.
    The least likely item is insecticide, which is used by 58
    per cent. (Source, British Market Research Bureau.)

Health

1 How many times does the average British male consult his family doctor in a year?

(a) 21 times
(b) 12 times
(c)   3 times

2 Does it cost the National Health Service more to treat men or women?

3 Currently, some 99 per cent of live births take place in hospital. Where do most stillbirths occur?

(a) In hospital
(b) Elsewhere

4 Private patients generally stay longer in National Health Service hospitals than patients being treated entirely under the NHS. True or false?

Against which of these diseases are we most likely to immunize our babies?

(a) Measles
(b) Whooping cough
(c) Rubella

Answers Health

1   The average British male consults his doctor 3.5 times a
     year. The largest number of visits is made by the under-
     fives (7.2), and the smallest number by the 16-44s (2.2).
     (Source, *General Household Survey*.)

2   It costs more to treat women each year (average cost in
     1981, £222) than men (£192). (Source, Central Statistical
     Office.)

3   Most stillbirths occur in hospital. Only about 2.5 per cent
     occur elsewhere. (Source, Department of Health and
     Social Security.)

4   It is false. Private patients generally have a shorter stay.
     This reflects the fact that private patients are often
     admitted for conditions needing short-term treatment.
     (Source, *Social Trends,* 1984.)

5   We are most likely to immunize our babies against
     measles. In 1982, 56 per cent of children born in 1980 had
     been immunized against measles, compared with 52 per
     cent against whooping cough. Rubella immunization is now
     generally given to children under the age of ten. (Source,
     Department of Health and Social Security.)

Sickness

Which are we most likely to suffer from in a 12-month period?

(a) Headaches
(b) Catarrh
(c) Indigestion
(d) Rheumatism
(e) Coughs

Which of these diseases is *not* on the increase?

(a) Infective jaundice
(b) Typhoid
(c) Whooping cough

Which group is more likely to suffer from chronic sickness, drinkers or teetotallers?

If you are under 35, you are statistically most likely to die from an accident, or other violent means. If you're 50 and over, it's likely to be heart disease. What kills those in between?

Where should you move to in England to lessen your chances of dying of cancer?

(a) West Yorkshire
(b) Greater London
(c) Tyneside
(d) The Isle of Wight

Answers Sickness

1 We are most likely to suffer from headaches – some 58 per cent of adults claim to have had a headache at some time during a year. 50 per cent of us get coughs, 32 per cent indigestion, 23 per cent catarrh and 12 per cent rheumatism. (Source, British Market Research Bureau.)

2 Typhoid is the only one of these diseases that is not on the increase. Whooping cough increased from 4,400 cases in 1976 to 70,900 in 1982. Infective jaundice rose from 7,600 cases in 1976 to 12,000 cases in 1982. (Source, Office of Population Censuses and Surveys.)

3 Teetotallers are more likely than drinkers to suffer from chronic sickness. This is true throughout almost the whole age range for both men and women. The reasons for this could either be that moderate drinking is good for your health, or that people who are chronically sick have given up drinking because of their health. (Source, *General Household Survey*.)

4 Cancer is the most likely cause of death for people in the middle-age group. (Source, Office of Population Censuses and Surveys.)

5 It is best to move to West Yorkshire, which has one of the lowest rates of cancer mortality. London and Tyneside have some of the highest rates. (Source, *Atlas of Cancer Mortality in England and Wales, 1968-1978,* John Wiley, 1983.)

Disability

1   How many disabled people would a firm with 100
    employees be expected to take on under the law?

    (a)   None
    (b)   Three
    (c)   Seven

2   What percentage of adults in England and Wales have no
    natural teeth?

    (a)   43 per cent
    (b)   29 per cent
    (c)   7 per cent

3   What percentage of the adult population of Britain is
    reckoned to be illiterate?

    (a)   11 per cent
    (b)   6 per cent
    (c)   1 per cent

4   Is it true that more adults in Britain do wear glasses than
    don't?

5   What is the most common age group of drug addicts
    receiving treatment?

    (a)   15-19
    (b)   20-24
    (c)   30-34

Answers   Disability

1   It would normally have to take on three. The Disabled Persons (Employment) Act, 1944, requires employers with 20 or more employees to include 3 per cent registered disabled people in their workforce. (Source, Department of Employment.)

2   In England and Wales, 29 per cent of adults have no natural teeth. (Source, Office of Population Censuses and Surveys.)

3   Some 6 per cent of the adult population is reckoned to be illiterate, in the sense of not being able to read or write satisfactorily. (Source, British Association of Settlements.)

4   It is true. Glasses or contact lenses are worn by 56 per cent of men and 67 per cent of women aged over 16. (Source, *General Household Survey*.)

5   The most common age group of drug addicts receiving treatment in 1982 was 30-34. (Source, Department of Health and Social Security.)

Accidents

1   More people are killed each year working in the construction industry than in mining. True or false?

2   More than 100 people are killed on the roads in an average day in Britain. True or false?

3   If you have an accident and need an ambulance, where is the best place to be in England (in terms of vehicle numbers per head of population)?

    (a)   Cumbria
    (b)   Oxfordshire
    (c)   Hampshire
    (d)   Essex

4   Which is the most frequent cause of accidental death in the home?

    (a)   Electric shocks
    (b)   Poisoning
    (c)   Falls
    (d)   Fires

5   In which country are you most likely to have a motoring accident?

    (a)   United Kingdom
    (b)   Italy
    (c)   Holland

Answers Accidents

1 It is true – 102 in the construction industry in Britain in 1982 compared with 73 in mining. But the *rates* are very different, because there are more workers in construction. For every 100,000 at risk in construction, 10 were killed; in mining and quarrying, the figure was more than double this at 22 in 100,000. (Source, Health and Safety Executive.)

2 It is false. Approximately 17 people are killed on the roads in one average day. (Source, Office of Population Censuses and Surveys.)

3 Cumbria is the best place to be. With a total of 21 ambulances per 100,000 population, it is almost twice as well off as Oxfordshire, Hampshire and Essex, which each have 11 ambulances per 100,000 people. (Source, *Hansard*.)

4 Falls are the most frequent cause, accounting for more than 50 per cent of all accidental deaths in the home in Britain. (Source, Office of Population Censuses and Surveys.)

5 On the basis of mileage covered for every death or serious injury, the United Kingdom is the most dangerous country of the three, though statistically much safer than Belgium, Austria, Spain or Greece. (Source, AA/RAC.)

Vices

1   The population spends more on drink and tobacco in one
    year than the government spends on the National Health
    Service. True or false?

2   Women are now more likely than men to be cigarette
    smokers. True or false?

3   What is the most common daily cigarette consumption
    among smokers in Britain?

    (a)   Under 10
    (b)   10 to 19
    (c)   20 or over

4   It is estimated that some 94 per cent of adults gamble at
    some time or another. How many do it regularly?

    (a)   3 per cent
    (b)   21 per cent
    (c)   39 per cent

5   Which form of gambling attracts the most money in
    Britain?

    (a)   Bingo clubs
    (b)   Casinos and gaming clubs
    (c)   Local authority and society lotteries

Answers   Vices

1   It is true. In 1982 we spent approximately £18,000 million on drink and tobacco, compared with the £14,000 million spent by the government on the National Health Service. (Source, Central Statistical Office.)

2   False. Though men, over the past decade, have been giving up smoking at a faster rate than women, they still smoke more; 38 per cent of men smoke, compared with 33 per cent of women. (Source, *General Household Survey*.)

3   Nearly half the smokers in Britain (43 per cent) consume 20 or more cigarettes a day; 38 per cent smoke between ten and 19, and 19 per cent smoke fewer than ten. (Source, *General Household Survey*.)

4   Some 39 per cent of the adult population gamble regularly This definition of gambling, of course, includes the football pools. (Source, *Britain 1984*.)

5   Casinos and gaming clubs attract the most money – £1,007 million in the year ending mid-1982, compared with £464 million staked in bingo clubs and £78 million spent on lottery tickets. (Source, Home Office and Customs and Excise.)

Welfare

1   Which has the greatest number of clients?

    (a)   The National Marriage Guidance Council
    (b)   Alcoholics Anonymous
    (c)   The Samaritans

2   Who is more likely to receive the attention of a health visitor, a child under five or an adult over 65?

3   Which is the biggest source of problems taken to Citizens' Advice Bureaux?

    (a)   Consumer or business matters
    (b)   Housing issues
    (c)   Social security difficulties

4   Which of the following charities attracts the highest voluntary income?

    (a)   The RSPCA
    (b)   The National Trust
    (c)   The Spastics Society

5   On which does the government spend more, maternity benefit or war pensions?

Answers Welfare

1 The Samaritans have the greatest number of clients –
   319,000 in 1982, compared with some 40,000 for the
   National Marriage Guidance Council and 29,000 for
   Alcoholics Anonymous. (Source, *Social Trends,* 1984.)

2 Children under five account for most of the cases attended
   by health visitors – 59 per cent, compared with 13 per
   cent for the over-65s. (Source, Department of Health and
   Social Security.)

3 Consumer and trade matters are the biggest source of the
   4.5 million new inquiries that Citizens' Advice Bureaux
   get annually. They account for 17 per cent of the inquiries.
   (Source, *Social Trends,* 1984.)

4 The voluntary income of the National Trust was nearly
   three times that of the RSPCA or the Spastics Society in
   1983. (Source, Charities Aid Foundation.)

5 The government spends more on war pensions than on
   maternity benefit – £542 million in 1982-83, compared
   with £168 million. (Source, Central Statistical Office.)

Housing

1 Which kind of household, on average, pays out the most each week for their housing?

    (a) People buying with a mortgage (after tax relief)
    (b) People in privately rented furnished accommodation
    (c) Local authority tenants

2 Is it true that council houses are more likely to be burgled than owner-occupied houses?

3 Which cost more to buy, on average, new houses or secondhand ones?

4 More British households occupy semi-detached than terraced houses. True or false?

5 Which accounts for most of the housing in serious disrepair in England?

    (a) Council-owned housing
    (b) Owner-occupied housing
    (c) Privately rented housing

Answers Housing

1   People buying on a mortgage pay out most, even after tax
    relief is taken into account. They pay nearly twice as
    much, on average, as people in the next most expensive
    category, privately rented furnished accommodation.
    (Source, *Social Trends,* 1984.)

2   It is true that council houses are more likely to be burgled.
    It is also true that the highest burglary rate among socio-
    economic groups is for households headed by an unskilled
    worker. (Source, *General Household Survey.*)

3   New housing, on the whole, costs more than secondhand
    housing. The main exception is Greater London, where in
    several boroughs, older housing is more expensive.
    (Source, Abbey National Building Society.)

4   It is false. Fewer households are in semi-detached houses –
    31 per cent, compared with 32 per cent in terraced houses.
    (Source, *General Household Survey.*)

5   Owner-occupied housing, which accounts for 51 per cent
    of all dwellings in serious disrepair. (Source, English
    House Condition Survey, Department of the Environment.)

Energy

1 Thirty years ago, the United Kingdom imported almost its
entire oil requirement. Where does it stand now in the
world league of oil producers?

  (a) Fifth
  (b) Fifteenth
  (c) Twentieth

2 One of these fuels generates over half of the nation's
electricity. Which?

  (a) Oil
  (b) Coal
  (c) Nuclear fuels

3 The Northern Irish, per head of population, are the
greatest consumers of natural gas in the United Kingdom.
True or false?

4 For what purpose do we use most electricity in the home?

  (a) Water heating
  (b) Cooking
  (c) Heating the home

5 How much longer does the government reckon that coal
resources will last, at present rates of consumption and
using existing technology?

  (a) 300 years
  (b) 900 years
  (c) 3,000 years

Answers Energy

1   The United Kingdom is the world's fifth largest oil
    producer, producing some two million barrels of oil a day.
    (Source, Department of Energy.)

2   Coal generates more than two-thirds of our electricity.
    (Source, Central Electricity Generating Board.)

3   It is false. Natural gas is not supplied at all to Northern
    Ireland. (Source, Department of Energy.)

4   We use most domestic electricity (a quarter of total
    consumption) for water heating. One-fifth goes on home
    heating and one-tenth on cooking. (Source, Department
    of Energy.)

5   There are some 45,000 million tonnes of recoverable coal,
    which, by official estimates, should last another 300
    years. (Source, National Coal Board.)

Environment

1   Is the amount of agricultural land taken for development
    in the United Kingdom increasing or decreasing?

2   Who owns most of the woodlands in the United Kingdom?

    (a)   The state
    (b)   The church
    (c)   The landed aristocracy

3   Scotland has more common land than England and Wales
    put together. True or false?

4   Which accounts for more of the land area of England?

    (a)   Land used for crops
    (b)   Land used for grass
    (c)   Land that is built up or used for recreation

5   Which accounts for the greater total mileage, motorways
    or canals and navigable waterways?

Answers Environment

1   It is decreasing – from 45,000 acres a year between 1965 and 1970 to 23,000 acres a year between 1975 and 1980. (Source, *Britain 1984*.)

2   The state owns most of the woodlands in the United Kingdom – 52 per cent altogether. There are wide regional variations, however, with a figure of 85 per cent in Northern Ireland and 15 per cent in the North-west. (Source, *Regional Trends,* 1984.)

3   It is false. While England and Wales have some 1.5 million acres of common land, there is none in Scotland (or Northern Ireland). (Source, *Britain 1984*.)

4   Land used for grass (41 per cent) accounts for the greatest area, followed by crops (33 per cent) and built-up areas (18 per cent). (Source, Ministry of Agriculture, Fisheries and Food.)

5   Canals and navigable waterways account for the greater total mileage. About 2,000 miles are controlled by the British Waterways Board, while there are some 1,700 miles of motorway in the United Kingdom. (Source, Department of Transport.)

Pollution

1 Which is the biggest single cause of smoke pollution in the United Kingdom?

  (a) Stubble burning
  (b) Domestic open fires
  (c) Power stations

2 Where would you find the most polluted rivers in England and Wales?

  (a) Yorkshire
  (b) Wales
  (c) The North-west
  (d) The South-west

3 Which area of the United Kingdom suffers most from smoke in the atmosphere?

  (a) Northern Ireland
  (b) The north of England
  (c) The South-east
  (d) Greater London

4 About what sort of noise are we most likely to make an official complaint?

  (a) Noise from roadworks, demolition and construction
  (b) Noise from industrial and commercial premises
  (c) Noise from other people's houses

5 On average, do men or women have higher concentrations of lead in the blood?

Answers **Pollution**

1   Domestic open fires, which annually emit 0.24 million tonnes of smoke, are the biggest single cause of smoke pollution in the United Kingdom. (Source, Department of Trade and Industry.)

2   The most polluted rivers are in Yorkshire, according to a National Water Council survey in 1980. Yorkshire had 418 kilometres of 'grossly polluted' rivers, the North-west 311 kilometres, and the rest of England and Wales 253 kilometres. (Source, National Water Council.)

3   Northern Ireland has the worst concentration of smoke in the atmosphere, with levels about double those in South-east England. (Source, *Regional Trends,* 1984.)

4   We are most likely to complain about noise from other people's houses. Complaints about noise from domestic premises account for nearly 60 per cent of all complaints about noise received by environmental health officers in England and Wales. (Source, Institution of Environmental Health Officers.)

5   Almost all surveys find that men have higher concentrations of lead in the blood than women, though for women, concentrations tend to rise more steeply with age. (Source, *Social Trends,* 1984.)

Transport

A total of 43 per cent of households in Britain have one car or van. How many have more than one?

(a)   2 per cent
(b)   7 per cent
(c)   16 per cent

Which accounts for more of total passenger transport in Britain (in terms of passenger kilometres travelled)?

(a)   The bicycle
(b)   Air transport

At what time of day do most road casualties occur?

(a)   8 am
(b)   4 pm
(c)   11 pm

More people in Britain walk to work than travel by train. True or false?

Some two million driving tests are taken in Britain each year. The pass rate is 53 per cent for men. What is the percentage pass rate for women?

(a)   32 per cent
(b)   43 per cent
(c)   54 per cent

Answers Transport

1   A total of 16 per cent of households in Britain have more than one car or van. (Source, *General Household Survey*.)

2   The bicycle accounts for more passenger transport than the aeroplane – 1 per cent of total domestic transport, compared with 0.5 per cent. (Source, *Social Trends,* 1984.

3   Most road casualties in Britain occur between 4 pm and 5 pm. On the whole, higher casualty figures coincide with the times of day when traffic is heaviest. The exception is the hour between 11 pm and midnight, when there are more casualties than in the morning rush hour between 8 am and 9 am. (Source, Department of Transport.)

4   It is true. Professional workers are the most likely to use the train; walking is the commonest means of travel for unskilled workers. (Source, Office of Population Censuses and Surveys.)

5   The pass rate for women is 43 per cent. (Source, Department of Transport.)

Lifestyles

1 Most women who do a full-time job feel that their husbands do not do enough housework. True or false?

2 What is the trend in the number of couples who live together before marriage, compared with the early 1970s? Has it:

   (a) Stayed about the same?
   (b) Doubled?
   (c) Tripled?

3 How many adults never lock the lavatory door?

   (a)   4 per cent
   (b) 14 per cent
   (c) 43 per cent

4 Which are we more likely to use, shampoo or toothpaste?

5 More women than men own pet cats. Who is more likely to own a dog?

Answers Lifestyles

1 It is false. The survey, *Women and Employment,* published by the Department of Employment and the Office of Population Censuses and Surveys in 1984, found that 74 per cent of women working full-time thought what their husbands did was 'about right'. Only 21 per cent thought it was 'not enough'.

2 The number has almost tripled. A third of the women under 35 in Britain who married in the early 1980s had been cohabiting with their husbands. In 1970-74, the proportion was 13 per cent. (Source, *General Household Survey*.)

3 Some 43 per cent of adults never lock the lavatory door. (Source, Gallup, quoted in *The Gallup Report* by Norman Webb and Robert Wybrow, Sphere Books, 1982.)

4 We are more likely to use shampoo than toothpaste. Nearly 10 per cent of families never use toothpaste, whereas only 6.5 per cent of women and 7.5 per cent of men never use shampoo. (Source, British Market Research Bureau.)

5 Women are also more likely to be dog-owners. Some 27 per cent of British women aged 15 or over are dog-owners, compared with 26 per cent of men. (Source, *Social Trends,* 1984.)

Leisure

1 Do more foreign visitors come to Britain than Britons go abroad? Or is it the other way round?

2 Is it true that the British are less keen on visiting museums than the Icelanders?

3 Which is the job most commonly done by do-it-yourselfers?

   (a) Painting inside
   (b) Wallpapering
   (c) Painting outside
   (d) Putting up shelves

4 Adult non-fiction accounts for the largest proportion of public library stocks in the United Kingdom. But from what section of the library is the largest number of books issued?

   (a) Adult fiction
   (b) Adult non-fiction
   (c) Children's books

5 Which is the most popular tourist attraction?

   (a) Kew Gardens
   (b) Stonehenge
   (c) Shakespeare's birthplace

Answers Leisure

1 Nearly twice as many Britons (20 million) make trips abroad in one year as overseas visitors (11 million) come here. (Source, British Tourist Authority.)

2 It is true. On a basis of museum visits per 1,000 of the population, the British are thirty-fifth in the world league, behind such countries as Iceland, Bulgaria, Singapore and the Irish Republic. (Source, UNESCO.)

3 Painting inside is the job most commonly done by do-it-yourselfers. In a year, some 57 per cent do this job, compared with 40 per cent who do wallpapering, the next most popular job. (Source, British Market Research Bureau.)

4 Adult fiction accounts for by far the largest number of books issued – 60 per cent compared with just over 20 per cent for adult non-fiction. (Source, Chartered Institute of Public Finance and Accountancy.)

5 Kew Gardens is the biggest attraction, with some 900,000 visitors in 1983, compared with roughly 600,000 for Stonehenge and 500,000 for Shakespeare's birthplace. (Source, British Tourist Authority.)

Entertainment

1   Which age group accounts for the keenest readership of
    romantic fiction?

    (a)   16-34
    (b)   35-44
    (c)   55 and over

2   In 1951, there were some 4,600 cinemas in Britain. How
    many are there now?

    (a)   Half this number
    (b)   A quarter
    (c)   One-sixth

3   Which type of musical instrument sells best?

    (a)   Pianos
    (b)   Guitars and stringed instruments
    (c)   Electronic organs
    (d)   Wind instruments

4   The number of provincial theatres in Britain declined
    throughout the 1970s. True or false?

5   Which of these entertainment activities are we most likely
    to indulge in?

    (a)   Eating out
    (b)   Entertaining at home
    (c)   Visiting a pub or club.
    (d)   Reading books

Answers Entertainment

1   The keenest readers of romantic fiction are people of 55 and over. In a national survey in 1983, 23 per cent of over-55s who were reading a book described it as a romance. (Source, *The Book Report,* Euromonitor Publications.)

2   Roughly one-sixth of the 1951 figure. In 1982 there were some 800 cinemas with a total of 1,400 screens. (Source, Department of Trade.)

3   Electronic organs are the best-sellers, with 50 per cent of retail sales of musical instruments. Pianos have 20 per cent, and stringed instruments 10 per cent. (Source, Euromonitor.)

4   It is false. The number of provincial theatres in Britain increased between 1975 and 1981, from 295 to 331. (Source, British Theatre Directory.)

5   Reading books is the most popular activity – indulged by 51 per cent of people. Visits to pubs and clubs are next most popular (37 per cent), followed by entertaining at home (29 per cent) and eating out (17 per cent). (Source, Mintel/British Market Research Bureau.)

The arts

1   Which county has the greatest number of listed buildings per 100,000 population?

    (a)   Greater London
    (b)   Merseyside
    (c)   Staffordshire
    (d)   Wiltshire

2   Which of these authors has the biggest following today, as measured by the size of their official appreciation society?

    (a)   Dickens
    (b)   Agatha Christie
    (c)   Shaw
    (d)   Trollope

3   Who is the most popular playwright with English theatregoers outside London?

    (a)   Shakespeare
    (b)   Terence Rattigan
    (c)   Noel Coward
    (d)   Alan Ayckbourn

4   Excluding grants to the main national companies, which of the arts receives most money from the Arts Council?

    (a)   Music
    (b)   Drama
    (c)   Art
    (d)   Literature

5   Who is the favourite composer with operatic audiences in England and Wales?

    (a)   Wagner
    (b)   Verdi
    (c)   Puccini
    (d)   Mozart

Answers   The arts

1   Wiltshire has the most listed buildings per 100,000 population – 1,822, compared with Greater London's 453. (Source, English Tourist Board.)

2   The Dickens Fellowship is the largest of the societies in the United Kingdom devoted to particular authors. (Source, *Britain 1984.*)

3   The most popular playwright is Alan Ayckbourn. A total of 327,009 people outside London attended performances of his plays in 1982-83, compared with 318,000 for Shakespeare. (Source, Arts Council.)

4   Over the past decade music and drama have received most financial support from the Arts Council. In 1982-83, these accounted for 20 per cent and 19 per cent of the budget respectively. (Source, *Social Trends, 1984.*)

5   The favourite (in terms of numbers of performances by the main state-supported companies in 1982-83) is Mozart (97 performances) followed by Puccini (78 performances). (Source, Arts Council.)

Newspapers and magazines

1 Which of these periodicals has the highest number of readers per copy?

   (a) *TV Times*
   (b) *Woman*
   (c) *The Spectator*
   (d) *Country Life*

2 Which is the favourite daily national newspaper of people over 65?

3 We are more likely to read a daily newspaper than a Sunday paper – or is it the other way round?

4 What do the British prefer to read about in their magazines?

   (a) Sex
   (b) Women's topics
   (c) Do-it-yourself
   (d) Television listings

5 Which of the quality newspapers is most read by people in the unskilled working class?

   (a) *Financial Times*
   (b) *The Guardian*
   (c) *The Times*
   (d) *Daily Telegraph*

Answers   Newspapers and magazines

1   *Country Life* is estimated to have the highest number of readers per copy, about 25. (Source, *Social Trends,* 1984.)

2   *The Daily Mirror.* It is read by 17 per cent of people over 65, compared with 16 per cent for the *Sun* and 14 per cent for the *Daily Express.* (Source, *Social Trends,* 1984.)

3   We are, in fact, slightly more keen on Sunday newspapers. For example, 79 per cent of people in social class A read a national Sunday paper compared with 77 per cent reading a national daily newspaper. A similar differential is maintained throughout the class range. (Source, National Readership Survey.)

4   People who buy magazines prefer television listings. The most popular magazines in Britain are the *Radio Times* and the *TV Times*, each with a circulation of over three million and average readership of 21 per cent of the population aged 15 or over. (Source, *Social Trends,* 1984.)

5   The *Daily Telegraph*, which is read by 1 per cent of people in the unskilled working class. (Source, National Readership Survey.)

Radio and television

1 At what age are you likely to spend most time watching television?

  (a)   5-15
  (b)   16-19
  (c)   20-29
  (d)   65 and over

2 What is the peak hour for adults watching television?

3 A half of this radio network's listening is by people over 55 and two-thirds of it is by women. Which network is it?

  (a)   BBC local radio
  (b)   Radio 2
  (c)   Radio 4
  (d)   Independent local radio

4 The average person spends just over 20 hours a week tuned in, and 20 per cent of households have two or more receivers. What are we talking about – radio or television?

5 Men spend more time watching television than do women. True or false?

Answers   Radio and television

1   You are likely to spend most time watching television between the ages of five and 15. (Source, BBC.)

2   The peak hour for adult television-viewing is 10 pm, when some 40 per cent are tuned in. (Source, BBC.)

3   It is Radio 4, which is the third most popular of the BBC radio networks, with a weekly patronage of 21 per cent of the population aged 12 or above. (Source, BBC.)

4   Television. The average time for radio-listening is half the television time, at just over ten hours a week. (Source, BBC.)

5   It is false. Women, both working and non-working, watch more television than men. (Source, BBC.)

Sport

1 There was a big increase during the 1970s in the numbers of people participating in sports. Which showed the largest increase, indoor or outdoor sports?

2 Which of these sports is the most popular among women in Britain?

   (a) Sailing
   (b) Tennis
   (c) Swimming
   (d) Horse riding

3 It's one of our fastest growing sports. Some 3.7 million people take part in it, more than two-thirds of whom are under 35. Most participants are skilled manual workers. What sport is it?

4 Which is more popular as a spectator sport, horse racing or motor racing?

5 Which of these sports is the odd one out in the way it is conducted in the United Kingdom today?

   (a) Rugby Union
   (b) Cricket
   (c) Rowing
   (d) Hockey

Answers   Sport

1   Indoor sport showed the greater increase – from 9 per cent
of the adult population taking part in 1973, to 23 per cent
in 1980. Outdoor sport is still more popular overall,
though with a slower growth rate, from 25 to 30 per cent.
(Source, *Britain 1984*.)

2   Swimming is the most popular sport. Some 6 per cent of
women take part in indoor swimming and 2 per cent in
outdoor swimming. (Source, Sports Council.)

3   Angling (Source, National Angling Survey.)

4   Motor racing is more popular than horse racing as a
spectator sport. Attendances in 1982 totalled four million,
compared with 3,700,000 for horse racing. (Source, Racing
Industry Statistical Bureau and RAC.)

5   Cricket is the odd one out. The other three are amateur
sports. (Source, *Britain 1984*.)

Holidays

1   When we take a holiday in Britain, what is the most common period spent away from home?

    (a)   Less than a week
    (b)   Between one and two weeks
    (c)   Two weeks and over

2   Where in the United Kingdom do we most favour going for our holidays?

    (a)   The South/South-east/Isle of Wight area
    (b)   The West Country
    (c)   Scotland
    (d)   North Wales/Isle of Man

3   Twenty years ago, the average manual worker was allowed two weeks holiday with pay. What is the average now?

4   Spain is the most popular destination for British holidaymakers going abroad. Which of these is second in popularity?

    (a)   France
    (b)   Greece
    (c)   Irish Republic

5   In which country are Britons abroad most likely to be robbed?

    (a)   The United States
    (b)   Italy
    (c)   France

Answers Holidays

1 More than half the holidays taken in this country by British residents last no more than a week, between four and seven nights. Over a quarter last between one and two weeks, but only one in 20 is longer than two weeks. (Source, *Britain 1984*.)

2 The West Country is marginally more popular as a holiday destination than the South/South-east. Scotland is next in popularity, followed by Wales/Isle of Man. (Source, British Market Research Bureau.)

3 The average amount of paid holiday for a manual worker is 4.2 weeks. (Source, Department of Employment.)

4 France is the second most popular destination, accounting for 15 per cent of holidaymakers, compared with Spain's 30 per cent. (Source, British Tourist Authority.)

5 Italy, particularly around Naples, is the place where Britons abroad are most likely to be robbed. (Source, Europ Assistance.)

Participation

1 Men are more likely to participate in sport, in general, than women. Which of the sports listed below has a greater female than male participation rate?

    (a) Cycling
    (b) Yoga and keep-fit
    (c) Tennis and squash
    (d) Horse riding

2 Some 3 to 4 per cent of the population participate in amateur music and drama. Who are they most likely to be?

    (a) Employers and managers
    (b) Middle grade white-collar workers
    (c) Students

3 Which of these organisations for young people has the most members?

    (a) The Brownies
    (b) The Sea Cadet Corps
    (c) The Boys' Brigade

4 How many people do voluntary work in Britain – that is, work for which they are not paid and which is of service to others, apart from their immediate family and friends?

    (a) One in 50
    (b) One in 17
    (c) One in 4

5 Which of these women's organisations has the largest membership?

    (a) The Mothers' Union
    (b) The National Federation of Women's Institutes
    (c) The National Union of Townswomen's Guilds

Answers **Participation**

1   Both horse riding and yoga and keep-fit have higher
    participation rates for women than for men. (Source,
    Social Trends, 1984.)

2   Students are most likely to participate in amateur music
    and drama. Of these, 13 per cent take part at some time,
    compared with 1 per cent of unskilled manual workers.
    (Source, *General Household Survey*.)

3   The Brownies have the most members – 419,000 in 1982,
    compared with 19,000 for the Sea Cadet Corps and 145,000
    for the Boys' Brigade. (Source, *Social Trends,* 1984.)

4   Approximately one in four people over 16 in Britain does
    some voluntary work over a period of one year. Women
    are more likely than men to take up such work. (Source,
    General Household Survey.)

5   The National Federation of Women's Institutes has the
    largest membership – 363,000 in 1982, compared with
    205,000 for the Mothers' Union and 175,000 for the
    National Union of Townswomen's Guilds. (Source, *Social
    Trends,* 1984.)

Trade unions

1   Union membership has been in decline since the end of the
    1970s. In which area of employment have the losses been
    greatest?

    (a)   Insurance, banking and finance
    (b)   Gas, electricity and water
    (c)   Textiles

2   Which area of employment is the most unionized?

    (a)   Public administration
    (b)   Private manufacturing
    (c)   Private services

3   Which of these unions has the most members?

    (a)   The Iron and Steel Trades Confederation
    (b)   The National Union of Mineworkers
    (c)   The National Graphical Association

4   In what proportion of workplaces are trade unions
    recognised by the management?

    (a)   One-third
    (b)   A half
    (c)   Two-thirds

5   What percentage of manual trade union members attend
    the branch meetings of their unions?

    (a)   3 per cent
    (b)   7 per cent
    (c)   34 per cent

Answers Trade unions

1   The losses have been greatest in textiles, where union
    membership declined by 47 per cent between 1979 and
    1981. (Source, Department of Employment.)

2   Public administration is the most unionized area. In 1980,
    89 per cent of workers in public administration were
    members of a trade union. The figures for private
    manufacturing and private services were 68 per cent and
    55 per cent respectively. (Source, *Workplace Industrial
    Relations in Britain,* by W.W. Daniel and Neil Millward,
    Heinemann Educational Books, 1983.)

3   The National Union of Mineworkers has most members
    (245,000 in 1983). The Iron and Steel Trades Confederation
    has least (95,493 in 1983). (Source, *Whitaker's Almanack.*)

4   Trade unions are recognised in some two-thirds of
    workplaces (67 per cent in 1980). (Source, *Workplace
    Industrial Relations in Britain,* by W.W. Daniel and Neil
    Millward, Heinemann Educational Books, 1983.)

5   About 7 per cent of manual union members attend their
    branch meetings. (Source, *Workplace Industrial Relations
    in Britain,* by W. W. Daniel and Neil Millward,
    Heinemann Educational Books, 1983.)

Religion

1 Which of these religious groups has the largest
representation in the United Kingdom?

   (a) Jews
   (b) Methodists
   (c) Members of the Church of Scotland
   (d) Baptists

2 Which age group is best represented among people
attending church on Sunday?

   (a) Under 15
   (b) 15-19
   (c) Over 65

3 Merseyside has the highest proportion of church members
in England (35 per cent). Which region has the lowest?

   (a) Humberside
   (b) Greater London
   (c) Greater Manchester

4 How many of us believe in the Devil?

   (a) 1 per cent
   (b) 3 per cent
   (c) 20 per cent

5 Which are we more likely to own, a bible or a dictionary?

Answers Religion

1   The Church of Scotland accounts for the largest group, with an adult communicant membership of some 919,000. There are some 500,000 Methodists, 400,000 Jews and 168,000 members of the Baptist Union. (Source, *Britain 1984*.)

2   The under-15s. Though they account for one-fifth of the total population in England, they account for a quarter of church attendance. (Source, Bible Society.)

3   Humberside has the lowest proportion of church members in England (9 per cent). (Source, Bible Society.)

4   Over 20 per cent of people in Britain say they believe in the Devil. (Source, Gallup, quoted in *The Gallup Report*, By Norman Webb and Robert Wybrow, Sphere, 1982.)

5   We are more likely to own a dictionary than a bible – 89 per cent of British households, compared with 84 per cent But there is a difference between classes – the semi-skilled and unskilled working classes are more likely to own a bible (79 per cent) than a dictionary (77 per cent). (Source, Gallup.)

Elections

1 All elections of political representatives in the United Kingdom operate on the 'first-past-the-post' system. True or false?

2 The lowest turnout in the United Kingdom in the 1983 general election was in a seat won by the Conservatives in an inner-city area. Which city?

(a) London
(b) Edinburgh
(c) Bristol
(d) Bradford

3 In the 1983 general election this political party performed best in the constituencies of Ogmore (South Wales), Lewes and Kensington (London). What party is it?

(a) The Social Democratic Party
(b) The Ecology Party
(c) The Loony Party
(d) The Socialist Party of Great Britain

4 The 'top ten' seats where the National Front gained their highest poll in the 1983 general election were all except one in London. In which city was the exception?

(a) Manchester
(b) Birmingham
(c) Newcastle
(d) Cardiff

5 Which of these people are not entitled to stand for parliament?

(a) Undischarged bankrupts
(b) Roman Catholic priests
(c) Police superintendents
(d) Church of Ireland ministers

Answers Elections

1   It is false. Elections to the Northern Ireland Assembly, and elections in Northern Ireland for the European Parliament, operate on a system of proportional representation. (Source, Central Office of Information.)

2   The lowest turnout (51 per cent) was in the constituency of City of London and Westminster South. (Source, *British Parliamentary Constituencies,* by Ivor Crewe and Anthony Fox, Faber, 1984.)

3   The Ecology Party. Its share of the vote in its best constituency, Ogmore, was 2.9 per cent. (Source, *British Parliamentary Constituencies,* by Ivor Crewe and Anthony Fox, Faber, 1984.)

4   The provincial city where the National Front achieved their highest poll was Manchester, where they took 1.7 per cent of the vote in the Manchester Central constituency. (Source, *British Parliamentary Constituencies,* by Ivor Crewe and Anthony Fox, Faber, 1984.)

5   None of them are allowed to stand for parliament, under the House of Commons Disqualification Act, 1975. (Source, *Britain 1984.*)

Parliament

1   How many members of the House of Commons and House
of Lords receive ministerial appointments in modern
governments in the United Kingdom?

   (a)   30
   (b)   40
   (c)   100

2   One of these well-known inner city districts is at the heart
of the parliamentary constituency with the highest
unemployment in the United Kingdom. Which is it?

   (a)   Toxteth
   (b)   Moss Side
   (c)   The Gorbals
   (d)   Brixton

3   The British parliamentary constituency with the highest
proportion of professionally qualified workers is in north
London. True or false?

4   Which has the larger number of parliamentary seats,
Wales or Northern Ireland?

5   There are some 1,200 members of the House of Lords.
What is the average daily attendance?

   (a)   560
   (b)   290
   (c)   43

Answers Parliament

1   Approximately 100 members of the House of Commons and House of Lords receive ministerial appointments. (Source, *Britain 1984*.)

2   It is Toxteth, which makes up the biggest part of the Liverpool Riverside seat, where unemployment in 1984 was over 35 per cent. (Source, *British Parliamentary Constituencies,* by Ivor Crewe and Anthony Fox, Faber, 1984.)

3   It is false. The constituency with the highest number of professionally qualified workers is Sheffield Hallam (33.9 per cent professional). Bristol West and Glasgow Hillhead are second and third. A north London constituency, Hampstead and Highgate, is fourth. (Source, *British Parliamentary Constituencies,* by Ivor Crewe and Anthony Fox, Faber, 1984.)

4   Wales has the larger number of parliamentary seats – 38 compared with Northern Ireland's 17. (Source, Central Office of Information.)

5   The average daily attendance in the House of Lords is 290 (Source, *Britain 1984*.)

The police

1   There are roughly 2,000 people for every doctor in general
    practice. How many people are there for every policeman?

    (a)   400
    (b)   2,000
    (c)   9,000

2   The Metropolitan Police have the worst detection rate in
    England and Wales. Which police force has the best?

    (a)   Gwent
    (b)   Dorset
    (c)   Thames Valley
    (d)   Dyfed-Powys

3   Are we statistically more likely to initiate contact with the
    police, or to find them making contact with us?

4   What is the most common reason for people making an
    approach to the police?

    (a)   Asking the time
    (b)   Asking directions
    (c)   Reporting a crime
    (d)   Reporting a traffic accident

5   The people of which social group are most likely to be
    arrested by the police?

    (a)   The unemployed
    (b)   The unskilled working class
    (c)   The skilled working class

Answers The police

1   There are approximately 400 people for every police
    officer in the United Kingdom. (Source, *Britain 1984*.)

2   Dyfed-Powys and Gwent have the best detection rates
    (57 per cent of the notifiable offences recorded by the
    police are cleared up). The Metropolitan Police have a
    16 per cent success rate. (Source, *Hansard*.)

3   We are more than twice as likely to make contact with the
    police as to find them getting in touch with us. (Source,
    British Crime Survey.)

4   The most common reason for approaching the police is
    simply to ask the way. This accounts for 23 per cent of
    total contacts. (Source, British Crime Survey.)

5   The unemployed are most likely to be arrested. Of a
    sample of people interviewed about their experiences
    over a 14-month period, 9 per cent of the unemployed
    said they had been arrested, compared with 2 per cent of
    skilled manual workers, the next largest category.
    (Source, British Crime Survey.)

Crime

1   In what proportion of homicide cases is the victim related to, or acquainted with the attacker?

    (a)   One-tenth
    (b)   A third
    (c)   Three-quarters

2   What is the average value of goods stolen by shoplifters?

    (a)   £2
    (b)   £32
    (c)   £211

3   In what proportion of robberies in England and Wales are firearms used?

    (a)   One in 1,000
    (b)   One in 100
    (c)   One in ten

4   How many criminal incidents noticed by members of the public are *not* reported to the police?

    (a)   One in 20
    (b)   One in ten
    (c)   Two in three

5   What is the most common means of killing in cases of homicide?

    (a)   Shooting
    (b)   Strangulation
    (c)   A sharp instrument
    (d)   A blunt instrument

Answers   Crime

1   In approximately three-quarters of all homicide cases, the victim is related to, or acquainted with the person suspected of the attack. (Source, Home Office.)

2   The average value of shoplifted goods in 1984 was £32. (Source, National Association for the Care and Resettlement of Offenders.)

3   Firearms are used in approximately one in ten of the robberies recorded in England and Wales. (Source, Home Office.)

4   Approximately two in three criminal incidents that come to the attention of the public are not reported to the police. The main reason given is that they are too trivial. (Source, British Crime Survey.)

5   The most common means of killing in homicide cases recorded in England and Wales is a sharp instrument. (One in three cases.) (Source, Home Office.)

Prisons

How many Wembley Stadiums would you need to contain all the people who are given immediate prison sentences in England and Wales in one year?

What is the average 'stretch' for a man given an immediate prison sentence in England and Wales?

(a) One month
(b) Ten months
(c) Ten years

Where, outside the United Kingdom, are there most British subjects in prison?

(a) West Germany
(b) Greece
(c) South Africa
(d) Turkey

What chance is there that a man who has served a prison sentence of 18 months will be convicted again within two years of his release?

(a) One in 100
(b) One in 25
(c) One in 2

Prisoners serving fixed sentences of more than 18 months become eligible for release on parole after one-third, or 12 months, of their sentence. How many prisoners granted parole in England and Wales get recalled to prison?

(a) One in 9
(b) One in 18
(c) One in 80

Answers **Prisons**

1 One stadium would be adequate. A total of 56,000 people were given immediate prison sentences in England and Wales in 1982. A cup final crowd at Wembley can consist of up to 100,000 people. (Source, Home Office, *Daily Telegraph*.)

2 The average sentence (not including life sentences) is ten months. (Source, Home Office.)

3 In 1984 there were 200 British subjects in prison in West Germany, compared with 13 in Greece, 39 in South Africa and eight in Turkey. (Source, *Hansard*.)

4 A man who has served an 18-month prison sentence stands a one-in-two chance of being reconvicted within two years of his release. (Source, Home Office.)

5 Approximately one prisoner in nine (11 per cent) granted parole in England and Wales is recalled to prison. (Source *Britain 1984*.)

The courts and sentencing

There are some 50 million people in England and Wales.
How many receive a sentence from the courts in one year?

(a)   5,000
(b)   500,000
(c)   Two million

Which group of the population is most likely to be
cautioned by the police or found guilty in court of an
indictable (i.e., more serious) offence?

(a)   Males aged 21 or over
(b)   Females of all ages
(c)   Males aged between 14 and 16
(d)   Males aged between 17 and 21

In 1982, 586,000 people in England and Wales were found
guilty of, or cautioned for, indictable offences. Which
crime accounts for the largest number of offenders?

(a)   Violence against the person
(b)   Theft and handling stolen goods
(c)   Sexual offences
(d)   Burglary

If you were found guilty of fraud or forgery, what type of
sentence would you be most likely to receive?

(a)   A fine
(b)   A custodial sentence
(c)   A community service order or other type of sentence

If you were sentenced in a magistrates' court and decided
to appeal, what would be your chances of success?

(a)   One in 2
(b)   One in 10
(c)   One in 30

Answers   The courts and sentencing

1   In 1982, two million people were sentenced by the courts in England and Wales, over half of them for motoring offences. (Source, Home Office.)

2   In proportion to their numbers in the total population of England and Wales, males aged between 14 and 16 are most likely to be cautioned or found guilty of an indictable offence. The figure is 7,700 males per 100,000 of the population in this age group. (Source, Home Office.)

3   Theft and handling of stolen goods account for the largest number of offenders (55 per cent), followed by burglary (15 per cent). (Source, Home Office.)

4   People aged 17 and over found guilty of fraud or forgery in England and Wales would be most likely to be fined (42 per cent of cases). In 28 per cent of cases a custodial sentence is given. (Source, Home Office.)

5   You would stand a one-in-two chance of having your sentence varied or quashed if you appealed against a magistrates' court decision in England or Wales. (Source, Home Office.)

Defence

1   The United Kingdom is the world's fourth largest exporter of arms, after the United States, the Soviet Union and France. What percentage of world arms exports does it account for?

    (a)   4 per cent
    (b) 14 per cent
    (c) 24 per cent

2   The United Kingdom spends the largest proportion of its gross national product on defence of any NATO country except the United States. Is this true?

3   Fitter, Fishbed, Flogger and Fencer are all part of the nuclear armoury held by NATO and the Warsaw Pact countries. What are they?

    (a) American missiles
    (b) British submarines
    (c) Soviet aircraft
    (d) French tanks

4   On what type of military hardware does the government spend most: land, sea or air equipment?

5   Which of these illnesses accounts for the greatest number of people being discharged from the armed forces?

    (a) Heart disease
    (b) Mental disorders
    (c) Genito-urinary diseases

Answers Defence

1   The United Kingdom's share of world arms exports is some 4 per cent. The United States and the Soviet Union each account for more than 30 per cent. (Source, Stockholm International Peace Research Institute.)

2   It is not true. Greece is the NATO country that spends the largest proportion of its GNP on defence (7.1 per cent). The United States takes second place (6.9 per cent) and the United Kingdom third (5.4 per cent). (Source, Ministry of Defence.)

3   They are Soviet land-based aircraft. (Source, Ministry of Defence.)

4   The government spends most on air equipment, for which the 1984/85 estimate was £3,304 million. Sea equipment was allotted £2,222 million and land equipment £1,705 million. (Source, Ministry of Defence.)

5   Mental disorders account for the greatest number of people being discharged – 106 in 1982, compared with 16 cases of heart disease and 9 of genito-urinary disease. (Source, Ministry of Defence.)

The regions

1   In which English county are people most likely to lack an indoor lavatory?

    (a)   Lancashire
    (b)   Leicestershire
    (c)   West Sussex
    (d)   Durham

2   East Anglia has the lowest rate of illegitimacy in the English regions. Which region has the highest?

    (a)   The South-east
    (b)   The West Midlands
    (c)   The North-west

3   They eat the most butter – consuming an average of 4.9 ounces per person per week, compared with a national average of 3.4 ounces. Who are they?

    (a)   The English
    (b)   The Scots
    (c)   The Welsh
    (d)   The Northern Irish

4   In one of these counties, the percentage of the population born outside the United Kingdom is more than five times that in any of the other three counties named. Which is it?

    (a)   Bedfordshire
    (b)   Northumberland
    (c)   The Scottish Islands region
    (d)   Cumbria

5   What percentage of the Welsh population speaks Welsh?

    (a)   5 per cent
    (b)   19 per cent
    (c)   35 per cent

Answers   The regions

1   Leicestershire has the highest proportion of households lacking an inside lavatory (4.5 per cent). West Sussex has the lowest (0.9 per cent). (Source, *Regional Trends, 1984.*)

2   The North-west has the highest, with an illegitimacy rate of some 18 per cent of all live births. This compares with East Anglia's 11 per cent. (Source, *Regional Trends, 1984.*)

3   The Welsh consume this larger average amount of butter – they are also top of the league in milk and cream consumption, with an average of 4.8 pints per person per week, compared with a national average of 4.4 pints. (Source, *Regional Trends, 1984.*)

4   Bedfordshire is the county with the largest percentage of its population born outside the United Kingdom (10.4 per cent). The proportions for the others are: Northumberland, 1.6 per cent; the Scottish Islands, 1.8 per cent; Cumbria, 1.8 per cent. (Source, *Regional Trends, 1984.*)

5   Some 19 per cent of the Welsh population speaks the Welsh language. Welsh speakers are mostly in the rural north and west of the country. (Source, *Britain 1984.*)

Northern Ireland

1 Households in Northern Ireland spend a higher proportion of their total expenditure on fuel, food, tobacco and clothing than is spent on these items elsewhere in the United Kingdom. Do they also spend more on alcohol?

2 Northern Ireland has the highest suicide rate of any part of the United Kingdom. True or false?

3 Which of these churches has the greatest denominational strength in Northern Ireland?

   (a) Roman Catholic
   (b) Presbyterian
   (c) Church of Ireland
   (d) Methodist

4 Who are more likely to get killed in connection with civil disturbances in Northern Ireland, civilians or members of the security forces and police?

5 What is Northern Ireland's biggest industry?

   (a) Shipbuilding
   (b) Textiles
   (c) Agriculture

Answers Northern Ireland

1   The Northern Irish spend a smaller proportion of their
    total expenditure on alcohol than elsewhere in the United
    Kingdom – £3.60 for the average household in 1981-82,
    compared with £6.10 in the United Kingdom as a whole.
    (Source, *Regional Trends,* 1984.)

2   It is false. Northern Ireland's male suicide rate is some 87
    per cent of the United Kingdom's as a whole. The female
    rate is 49 per cent, and is one of the lowest in Europe.
    (Source, *Regional Trends,* 1984, and Office of Health
    Economics.)

3   The Roman Catholic church has the greatest
    denominational strength in Northern Ireland. (Source,
    United Kingdom Facts, by Richard Rose and Ian
    McAllister, Macmillan, 1982.)

4   Civilians are more likely to get killed when there is civil
    disturbance. In 1982, 57 civilians died compared with 40
    members of the security forces and police. (Source,
    Northern Ireland Office.)

5   Agriculture is Northern Ireland's biggest industry,
    accounting for almost one-tenth of civil employment in
    the province. (Source, *Britain 1984.*)

The British in the EEC

1   The Irish have 15 seats in the European Parliament, the
    Belgians 24 and the Italians 81. How many does the
    United Kingdom have?

    (a)   53
    (b)   81
    (c)   94

2   Our main bone of contention with the EEC has been over
    agriculture policy. Which of the following fruit and
    vegetables are most likely to be destroyed because of over-
    production?

    (a)   Tomatoes
    (b)   Apples
    (c)   Peaches
    (d)   Pears

3   Which of these statements is true?

    (a)   The United Kingdom has more doctors per head of
          population than most other EEC countries.
    (b)   The United Kingdom has fewer doctors per head of
          population than most other EEC countries.

4   The British drink more tea per person than any other EEC
    nation. True or false?

5   Of the ten countries in the EEC, where does the United
    Kingdom rank in turnout at elections for the European
    Parliament?

    (a)   Sixth
    (b)   Ninth
    (c)   Tenth

Answers   The British in the EEC

1   The United Kingdom has 81 seats, as do France, West Germany and Italy. (Source, European Parliament Directorate General for Information and Public Relations.)

2   The EEC destroys thousands of tons of *all* these foodstuffs every year. Top of the list are peaches – 350,000 tons of them are withdrawn from the market, of which 80 per cent are destroyed. (Source, *Hansard*.)

3   The second statement is true. Most of the United Kingdom has some 100 to 130 doctors per 100,000 inhabitants, whereas in parts of West Germany and Northern Italy, the figure is above 300. (Source, *An Atlas of EEC Affairs,* by Ray Hudson, David Rhind and Helen Mounsey, Methuen, 1984.)

4   It is false. The Irish drink more tea – 131 ounces per person in one year, compared with 125 ounces in the United Kingdom. (Source, *The Book of International Lists*, by George Kurian, Macmillan, 1981.)

5   The United Kingdom ranks tenth, with turnouts for the 1979 and 1984 elections of 31 per cent and 32 per cent respectively. Belgium, at the top of the list, had turnouts of 91 per cent and 92 per cent. (Source, European Parliament Directorate General for Information and Public Relations.)

The British in the world

1 Where in the world, in areas outside the North Atlantic Treaty Organisation, does the United Kingdom maintain a military presence?

2 All these countries are major recipients of British aid. How do they rank in order of the amount of money each receives?

   (a)   India
   (b)   Zimbabwe
   (c)   Bangladesh
   (d)   Kenya

3 In which of these countries is the Queen not the head of state?

   (a)   New Zealand
   (b)   Papua New Guinea
   (c)   Tuvalu
   (d)   Ghana

4 Which of these island groups is not a British dependency?

   (a)   The Cayman islands
   (b)   The Virgin islands
   (c)   The Pitcairn islands
   (d)   The Maldive islands
   (e)   The Turks and Caicos islands

5 Scotland leads the world in the death rate from this disease. Sweden is second, Northern Ireland third, and England and Wales fourth. What is the disease?

Answers The British in the world

1   Britain has a military presence in the Falkland Islands, in Cyprus, and in Hong Kong, Belize and Brunei. (Source, *Britain 1984*.)

2   The order (ranked according to the money received in 1983) is: India (£128 million); Kenya (£32 million); Bangladesh (£25 million); Zimbabwe (£20 million). (Source, Overseas Development Administration.)

3   The Queen is not head of state in Ghana. She is head of state in 18 countries altogether, including the other three listed in the question. (Source, *Britain 1984*.)

4   The Maldives are not a British dependency, they are an independent republic. (Source, *The Statesman's Yearbook*, 1984.)

5   Heart disease. It is responsible for more than 400 deaths in Scotland for every 100,000 of the population. (Source, World Health Organisation.)

Ethnic groups

1 How many households in Britain are headed by a person
   born outside the United Kingdom?

   (a) One in 14
   (b) One in 20
   (c) One in 52

2 Which is the largest ethnic or national minority group in
   the United Kingdom?

   (a) People from the Republic of Ireland
   (b) West Indians
   (c) Indians

3 Who are more likely to own their own houses?

   (a) Whites
   (b) People of Indian/Bangladeshi/Pakistani origin
   (c) People of West Indian or Guyanese origin

4 Which group of immigrants has the highest fertility rate
   (births per thousand women aged 15-44)?

   (a) Irish
   (b) Indian/Bangladeshi/Pakistani
   (c) West Indian

5 Some 6 per cent of white males in Britain have jobs of
   professional status. Is the percentage among men of
   Indian, Pakistani or Bangladeshi origin higher or lower?

Answers Ethnic groups

1   One in 14 households is headed by a person born outside the United Kingdom. The majority of these households are headed by someone born in the New Commonwealth and Pakistan. (Source, Office of Population Censuses and Surveys.)

2   The Irish are the largest single minority group in Britain. (Source, *Britain 1984.*)

3   People of Indian/Bangladeshi/Pakistani origin are most likely to be owner-occupiers. About 75 per cent of households in Britain headed by a person of Indian/Bangladeshi/Pakistani origin are owner-occupied, compared with a figure of 55 per cent for whites and 37 per cent for West Indian and Guyanese. (Source, Office of Population Censuses and Surveys.)

4   The highest fertility rate is among women of Indian/Pakistani/Bangladeshi origin. There are 160 births per thousand women in this group, compared with 60 for women of a similar age group born in the United Kingdom. The figure for both Irish and West Indian-born women is 65 per thousand. (Source, Office of Population Censuses and Surveys.)

5   It is more. Approximately 8 per cent of men in Britain who are of Indian/Pakistani/Bangladeshi origin have jobs of professional status. (Source, Department of Employment.)

Women

1 In 1984, there were 23 women MPs in the House of Commons. What is the highest number of women to have sat as Members of Parliament at any one time?

2 Forty-one per cent of male workers in Britain have dependent children. Are female workers more or less likely to have dependent children?

3 Which of these occupations is the biggest employer of women?

(a) Secretarial work and typing
(b) Selling
(c) Nursing
(d) Clerical work

4 Which of these professions has the greatest proportion of women members?

(a) Architects
(b) Surgeons
(c) Barristers
(d) Chartered accountants

5 What proportion of working women are in jobs which, at their place of work, are carried out exclusively by women?

(a) One in 50
(b) One in ten
(c) Two in three

Answers Women

1   The highest number of women MPs to have sat in the
    House of Commons at one time was 28 in 1964. (Source,
    The Times Guide to the House of Commons.)

2   Female workers are more likely (47 per cent) to have
    dependent children than are male workers. (Source,
    Labour Research.)

3   Clerical work is the largest area of employment for women
    in Britain, followed by cleaning and catering. Nearly 1.5
    million women work in clerical jobs. (Source, *Labour
    Research.*)

4   Barristers have the best female representation – with 10
    per cent of women in their ranks. The figures for the other
    professions are: architects, 7 per cent; accountants, 4 per
    cent; surgeons, less than 1 per cent. (Source, Equal
    Opportunities Commission and Royal Institute of British
    Architects.)

5   Some two in three working women (63 per cent) have jobs
    which are only done by women at that place of work. In
    certain employment areas, such as manufacturing, the
    figure is as high as four in five. (Source, *Women and
    Employment,* published by the Department of Employment,
    and the Office of Population Censuses and Surveys, 1984.)

Love and sex

1 What proportion of single women have had sexual intercourse by the age of 19?

   (a) One-tenth
   (b) A quarter
   (c) A half

2 Of the sexual offences recorded by the police in England and Wales, which category is the most common?

   (a) Homosexual offences
   (b) Unlawful intercourse with a girl under 16
   (c) Indecent assault on a female
   (d) Rape

3 Where are we most likely to meet a future spouse?

   (a) At a dance
   (b) At a pub
   (c) On a blind date
   (d) At college or university
   (e) At work

4 Despite the scares, the pill is the most popular type of contraceptive in Britain. Which is the second most popular?

5 Of every 1,000 teenage girls in Britain how many become pregnant in one year?

   (a) 40
   (b) 70
   (c) 200

Answers   Love and sex

1   More than half the single women in the United Kingdom
   have had sexual intercourse by the age of 19. The same is
   true of two-thirds of single men. (Source, *The Way Young
   People Learned about Sex,* by C. Farrell, Routledge and
   Kegan Paul, 1978.)

2   Indecent assault on a female is most common, accounting
   for more than half of all recorded sexual offences. (Source
   Home Office.)

3   We are most likely to meet our future spouse at a dance.
   Pubs and work are also important venues, though much
   depends on class. Women of higher social class are more
   likely, for example, to meet their future spouses at
   college. (Various sources, including *Sex and Generation,*
   by Diana Leonard, Tavistock, 1980.)

4   The sheath. There are 2.8 million sheath users, compared
   with 3.5 million women on the pill. (Source, Family
   Planning Association.)

5   Some 200 teenage girls out of 1,000 become pregnant each
   year. Of this total, 40 are already married. (Source, Birth
   Control Trust.)

The consumer society

1 On which do consumers in the United Kingdom spend more, alcohol or fuel?

2 More than £3,000 million a year is spent on advertising. Of the media listed here, one accounts for more of this total than all the rest put together. Which is it?

   (a) The press
   (b) Television
   (c) Commercial radio
   (d) Posters

3 Which of these items are we *least* likely to own?

   (a) A bicycle
   (b) A typewriter
   (c) A cigarette lighter
   (d) A sewing machine
   (e) A fountain pen

4 Ownership of which of these consumer durables showed the greatest increase over the decade from 1971 to 1981?

   (a) Cars
   (b) Television sets
   (c) Central heating
   (d) Washing machines

5 Which are you more likely to find in the average British home, a deep-freeze or a video recorder?

Answers The consumer society

1   We spend more on alcohol (£12,275 million in 1982) than on fuel (£8,731 million). (Source, Central Statistical Office.)

2   The press accounts for most of the money – 64 per cent, compared with 30 per cent for television, 2 per cent for commercial radio and 4 per cent for posters. (Source, *Britain 1984.*)

3   We are least likely to own a typewriter. Only 20 per cent of adults own one, compared with nearly 30 per cent who own a fountain pen. The most popular item on the list is a sewing machine, owned by 35 per cent of people. (Source, British Market Research Bureau.)

4   Ownership of central heating, which almost doubled over the decade. By 1981 it was installed in 60 per cent of households, as compared to 32 per cent in 1971. Ownership of television sets, already a high percentage, showed the smallest increase over the same period, from 91 per cent of households to 97 per cent. (Source, *Britain 1984.*)

5   A deep-freeze, even though the British have one of the highest rates for ownership of video recorders in the world. About 57 per cent of households have a deep-freeze, compared with some 18 per cent with a video recorder. (Source, *General Household Survey* and British Videogram Association.)

Books

Some useful sources of further information:

Social Trends, compiled annually by the Central Statistical Office, and published by Her Majesty's Stationery Office. A comprehensive digest of the most important social statistics of the day, accompanied by easy-to-read charts and diagrams. The figures are leavened by a highly readable commentary, which helps to explain the statistics and put them in context.

Annual Abstract of Statistics, compiled by the Central Statistical Office, and published by Her Majesty's Stationery Office. A stodgier though more comprehensive publication than *Social Trends.* All the vital (and not-so-vital) statistics about the United Kingdom are set out in tabular form, but with no diagrams and little commentary. A mine of information, even so.

Regional Trends, compiled annually by the Central Statistical Office and published by Her Majesty's Stationery Office. Comparisons of regional data of all kinds. This book will tell you almost anything about social life in the various parts of the country, from who eats the most potatoes, to where people drive the oldest cars.

Britain 1984, the government's annual official handbook, published by Her Majesty's Stationery Office. Thousands of facts about Britain and the British, but, inevitably, it tends to look on the rosy side. It makes more of test-tube babies and invisible exports than sewage on the beaches or lead in the blood.

General Household Survey, conducted by the Office of Population Censuses and Surveys and published by Her Majesty's Stationery Office. This is an annual government survey of a representative sample of households in Britain. It provides very detailed information on population, housing, family life, health and so on, and analyses the social changes that have taken place compared with previous years. A good complement to *Social Trends,* which reproduces some of its findings.

Whitaker's Almanack, published annually by Joseph Whitaker and Sons, is an eclectic selection of information, ranging from the times of high tide in Albert Dock, Hull, to the salary of the Archbishop of Canterbury. It is worth looking here for the sort of material, both British and foreign, that you can't find anywhere else.

The Statesman's Yearbook, published annually by Macmillan, is an A-Z of the history, demography and politics of all the nations of the world. It has details about everything from the number of telephones in Afghanistan to the size of the cassava crop in Zaire.

Most of these books are, regrettably, rather expensive, but in a town of any size, the library will almost certainly stock some or all of them.